12 au 15
janvier 1978

A ta petite hive, en souvenir
de notre merveilleuse halte à froid à
à Erie; il faisait très froid à
l'extérieur, mais si chaud au
cœur à l'intérieur... que ce ne
te rappelle notre échange
cettes et de souvenirs.
Merci, et que Dieu garde
ta belle famille —
Att! ♥
André
Olia ✗

COUNTRY COOKING

By The Editors of
Southern Living Magazine
Under the Direction of
Lena Sturges, Foods Editor

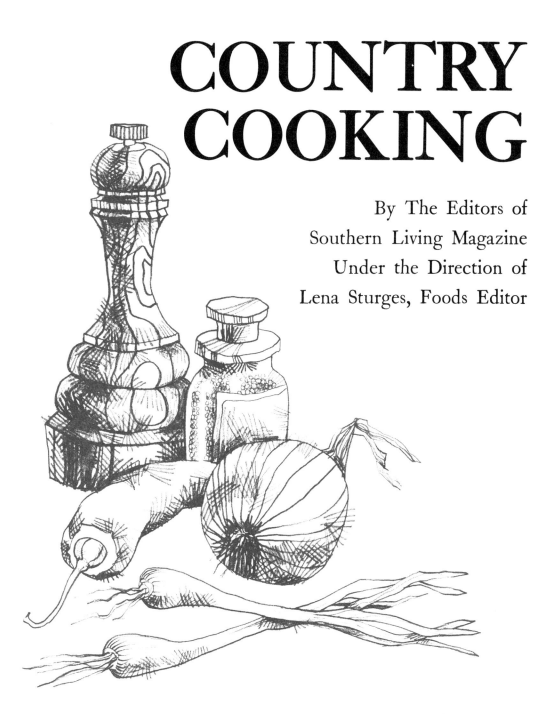

GALAHAD BOOKS · NEW YORK CITY

Introduction

When the "soul food" fad swept the country, Southerners smiled and said, "Why, that's just staple food."

Black-eyed peas and pot likker, collard greens and pigs' feet were born of hard times when any edible green and every part of an animal from head to feet and the "chitlins" in the middle were about all that was available.

Ingenuity transformed them into dishes as desirable as they were expedient. In fact, many of these traditional Southern foods make up what has been described as the first genuinely American cuisine utilizing native foods.

In times past, pork, corn, and wild greens predominated, and filled not only the dinner plate but dietary needs as well. Even if they were served every day, the variety of greens available — kale, collard, turnip, mustard, and dandelion — provided at least some change of pace.

Sweet potatoes have long had a place on the Southern menu. From biscuits to cake and pie, sweet potatoes appeared on the table just as often as greens and in innumerable forms.

Necessity was the mother of this cuisine which is still very much a part of today's prosperous South.

This compilation of over 500 kitchen-tested, farm-fresh recipes were selected from the more than 1,400 recipes featured in our SOUTHERN COUNTRY COOKBOOK. The original hardcover volume was first published in 1972 and was greeted by tremendous applause from folks all across the South. We believe this selection of recipes represents the very best of our native cuisine.

Copyright © 1974 by Oxmoor House, Inc., Book Division of the Progressive Farmer Company, P. O. Box 2463, Birmingham, Alabama 35202.

Published by arrangement with Oxmoor House, Inc.
Library of Congress Catalog Card Number: 74-23190
ISBN: 0-88365-2587

Manufactured in the United States of America

First Printing 1974

Contents

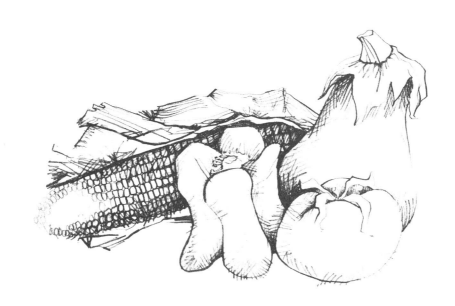

Sassafras Tea

Wash the sassafras roots, cut into
2- to 3-inch pieces; place in a deep pan,
cover with cold water, and boil for
about 12 to 15 minutes. Strain and serve
hot. Add lemon and sugar, if desired.
The tea is a delicate pink and is deli-
cious as a cold beverage.

*Note: Sassafras tea may be substituted for 1 cup
of liquid in plain cakes. Use a strong brew as a
flavoring for desserts and candies.*

Hog's Head Cheese

Prepare meat as for souse. Remove all
bones, and run meat through food chopper. For 5 pounds meat, use the
following:

2 *cups broth in which meat was boiled*
5 *teaspoons salt*
3 *teaspoons black pepper*
3 *teaspoons red pepper*
3 *teaspoons ground allspice*
2 *teaspoons ground cloves*

Mix thoroughly. Put into pans and press
with weight overnight. Head cheese may
be sliced, covered with vinegar, and
stored in glass jars. Yield: about
6 pounds.

Crackling Bread

2 *cups self-rising cornmeal*
2 *cups crisp cracklings, cut into size of
    large lima bean
    Boiling water
    Shortening to grease skillet
    All-purpose flour*

Put cornmeal into large mixing bowl,
add cracklings, and mix thoroughly.
Add enough boiling water to make a
medium stiff dough. Heat a well greased
iron skillet, sprinkle liberally with flour,
and pour in dough. Bake in a preheated
450° oven for 25 minutes or until brown.
Serve hot. Yield: about 6 to 8 servings.

Breadcrumb Pancakes

1 *tablespoon butter or margarine*
1½ *cups buttermilk*
1 *cup dry breadcrumbs*
2 *eggs*
½ *cup all-purpose flour*
1 *teaspoon soda*
½ *teaspoon salt*
½ *cup blueberries or strawberries*

Melt butter or margarine, add to milk,
and pour over crumbs. Add well beaten
eggs and dry ingredients sifted together.
Mix well. Add blueberries. Drop by
tablespoonfuls onto hot, greased griddle. Small cakes are easier to manage.
Yield: about 6 servings.

Cush

2 *tablespoons meat drippings*
2 *tablespoons butter*
3 *cups crumbled cornbread*
2 *cups crumbled biscuits*
   Salt and pepper to taste
1 *teaspoon ground sage*
1 *chopped onion*
2 *eggs*
   Milk

Heat meat drippings and butter in a
heavy skillet. Add cornbread and biscuits, salt and pepper, sage, onion, and
eggs. Stir and brown lightly. Then add
milk to make a soft, mushy batter and
cook until fairly dry. Cush may be
baked at 350° for about 15 to 20
minutes. Yield: 4 to 6 servings.

Fried Salt Pork

"Fat back," "poor man's chicken," or
whatever, the meat should be selected
with care. A streak of lean is most preferred, although many discriminating
cooks use the pure fat.

Allow 3 or 4 slices for each serving.
Use only thick slices. Cover with boiling

water, bring to a boil, discard the salt water. Drain, and dip slices in cornmeal. Fry in hot shortening until slices are golden brown. Drain on a paper towel. Serve with milk gravy, sliced tomatoes, or fried green tomatoes.

Often served for breakfast, the fried pork may also be served for patio or outside suppers.

To make milk gravy, pour off drippings, leaving about 2 tablespoons in frying pan. Add 2 tablespoons flour, and stir until brown. Add 2 cups milk slowly; stir and cook slowly until gravy is done. Serve with hot spoon cornbread, hot biscuits, cornbread, grits, or hominy.

Chitterlings

First, split the intestines. Then clean thoroughly in several changes of warm water. Soak overnight in salt water made by adding 1 teaspoon salt to 1 quart water. Cut into 2-inch lengths. Boil until tender. Dip in a light batter made of 1 egg, flour, and milk; or roll in meal, and fry.

Scrapple

1 pound pork
4 cups water
2 teaspoons salt
⅔ cup cornmeal
1 large onion
 Pepper
2 to 3 teaspoons ground sage

Cook meat, covered, in boiling salted water at simmering until meat falls from bones. Remove meat from broth. Cut or grind into small pieces. Strain broth into top of a double boiler. Add cornmeal, and cook over direct heat for 5 minutes, stirring constantly to prevent lumping. Add meat, chopped onion, and season to taste. Cook over boiling water for 1 hour. Pack into mold or small loafpans. Serve cold, or slice and pan fry with or without batter.

This South Carolina Scrapple recipe is typical, although some lean beef is often added to the pork. Often the broth from boiled meat from head cheese or souse is thickened and cooked with cornmeal, seasonings, and onion.

Liver Pudding

1 pound liver
½ hog's head
1 large onion
 Salt, red and black pepper
 Sage to taste

Dress and cook liver and hog's head until very tender. Remove hog's head meat from bones, and grind with liver and onion. Add seasonings. Press into mold and chill. May be served with grits or hominy or used in sandwiches. Yield: 6 servings.

Pig's Feet

Dress pig's feet and tie each separately in cheesecloth. Cover with boiling water. Season with 1 teaspoon salt for each quart of water. Simmer for about 4 hours, or until feet are tender. Serve feet cold with salt, pepper, and French salad dressing. Or split in half, dip in batter, and fry. Boiled pigs' feet may be pickled and served.

Pigtail with Turnip Greens

Clean pigtail thoroughly, salt to taste, and brown in shortening. Add about 1 cup water, cover and simmer slowly until tender, about 1½ to 2 hours. Serve with turnip greens.

Lye Hominy

Use 8 cups sweet, flat corn. (Most early varieties of sweet corn have the flat kernels.) Dissolve 2 ounces of concentrated lye in 1 gallon of boiling water in an iron kettle. Drop corn into this solution and boil rapidly for 25 to 30 minutes. Drain and put into a pot of cold water. If possible, allow water to run over it for 3 to 4 hours to remove all traces of lye. If this isn't possible, wash through about six changes of fresh water. After this, place in a barrel churn and turn the churn for 5 to 10 minutes to remove hulls and black eyes. After removing the hulls, place the corn in an enamel kettle, cover with clear boiling water, and cook until tender. Wash again and remove any hulls or eyes that failed to come off in the churn. The hominy may now be seasoned for serving. Yield: about 1 gallon.

Green Corn Pie

Grate several ears of green corn on a potato grater, enough to make about 3 cups of mush (the corn may be a little older and less tender than for roasting). Add the yolks of 2 eggs, a large spoonful of butter, pepper and salt, and the juice of 6 to 8 tomatoes scalded and pressed through a colander. Mix all well. Have ready young chickens stewed, as for chicken pie, or slices of cold veal and ham, or shrimp, or whatever you choose. Line a baking dish with half the batter, put the meat in the center, cover

with rest of batter, and bake at 325° for half an hour. Yield: about 6 servings.

To make corn fritters: Keep back several spoonfuls of the above batter, add 1 egg, a little more salt, and the grains of 4 or 5 ears of parboiled young corn, cut from the cob. Mix together and fry as fritters.

Poke Greens (or Sallet)

Poke greens for 4 to 6 servings
4 *thick slices bacon*
¾ *to 1 teaspoon salt*
12 *tender young onions, chopped*
2 *hard-cooked eggs, chopped*

Select tender, young poke greens. Clean thoroughly and rinse three times. Parboil twice and discard water. This is a most important step. Cover with water in large kettle and cook until greens are tender but not mushy. Fry bacon until crisp; remove from drippings, and set aside. Add poke greens, salt, and chopped onions to drippings. Cook over low heat for 20 minutes. To serve, sprinkle crumbled bacon and chopped hard-cooked eggs over greens. Yield: 4 to 6 servings.

Corncob Jelly

12 *medium red corncobs*
2 *quarts water*
1 *(1¼-ounce) package powdered pectin*
3 *cups sugar*

Wash the corncobs and cut into 4-inch lengths. Put into container, add 2 quarts water, and bring to a boil. Reduce heat and boil slowly for 35 to 40 minutes.

Strain the juice. Measure 3 cups of juice into large container. Add the powdered pectin and bring to a boil. Add sugar and again bring to the boiling point.

Boil for 5 minutes. Skim, and pour into hot, sterilized glasses or jars, and seal. Yield: about 5 pints.

Transparent Pudding

Lay in a deep dish any kind of dried sweetmeats. Rub ½ pound butter and ½ pound sugar together; beat 8 eggs well, and add them; then pour this mixture upon the sweetmeats, and bake in a 300° oven for 30 minutes. Turn it out of the dish, so that the preserves are at the top of the pudding. When quite cold, ice it; and it may be garnished to suit the fancy of the cook.

Pear Waffle Syrup

> 4 cups sweetened juice from
>   canned pears
>   Juice of 1 lemon
> 1½ (2½-ounce) packages
>   powdered pectin

Add lemon juice to pear juice and bring to a boil. Add fruit pectin and let come to a full rolling boil. Pour into jars immediately. Yield: 4 cups.

Canned Boiled Peanuts

Select well filled out "boiling peanuts" and wash them. Bring to a boil. Put peanuts into quart jars to within ½ inch of top of jar. Fill jars with boiling water and add 2 tablespoons salt to each jar. Cook at 10 pounds pressure for 30 minutes. Cool and store.

Vinegar Cobbler

Mix sugar, water, and vinegar to taste. Bring to a boil. Roll biscuit dumplings very thin and cut into strips. Drop into boiling liquid, cover pan and cook for about 15 minutes.

Boiled Peanuts

Select and wash young, green peanuts in the shell. Add 1 tablespoon salt to each quart of water, and boil peanuts for 2½ to 3 hours.

Barbecued Goat

Dress goat carefully. If hair gets in contact with meat, it imparts an unpleasant flavor. Add salt, pepper, chili powder, cumin seed, and cover goat with a layer of lard. Wrap and tie meat in maguey leaves. Cover with clean white sack and wrap in a tow sack. Put in pit where fire has been burning several hours. Lay covered meat in a layer of ashes over hot coals, cover with dirt, and leave meat in ashes all night.

Dried Whole Persimmons

Select fully ripened persimmons; rinse, drain, and place them about ¼ inch apart on a wire or cheesecloth frame, and dry in the sun. A fruit evaporator may be used, if preferred. When properly dried, the persimmons resemble dates in texture. Pack the dried fruit in glass jars which have been sterilized and then dried in a warm oven. Seal tightly and store in a cool, dry place.

Fried Pumpkin or Squash Blooms

Gather the blossoms while they are still in the large bud just ready to open. Wash carefully and press together flat. Dip in eggs, then in cornmeal or cracker crumbs. Add salt and pepper to taste. Fry in hot shortening until brown. Serve as a vegetable fritter.

Sandwich Suggestions

Fresh or day-old bread is usually better for sandwiches. For very thin slices, freeze the bread, and slice before it thaws.

When making sandwiches a day ahead, spread softened butter or margarine on slices before adding mayonnaise or salad dressing and filling. This will help keep the bread from becoming soggy. Spread filling to edge of bread. Crusts should be cut off (if desired) after filling has been spread so that sandwiches will retain their shape.

To keep openface or unwrapped sandwiches moist, cover with moisture-vaporproof material and place in refrigerator. Dainty sandwiches may be stacked several layers deep, if desired, but cover each layer with waxed paper. Never use a dampened towel to cover sandwiches.

Mix Hard-Cooked Eggs with:

Grated raw carrot, sliced ripe olives, mayonnaise
Chopped chicken, celery, onions, mayonnaise
Deviled ham, chopped pickles, mustard, mayonnaise
Tuna or salmon, celery, pickle relish, mayonnaise

Combine Cheese with:

Grated American cheese, dried beef, chili sauce
Bleu cheese, sliced turkey or ham
Swiss cheese slices, deviled ham, pickles
Cottage cheese, celery, green pepper
Sharp cheese spread, sliced salami, mustard

Use Chopped Chicken with:

Apple, celery, mayonnaise
Nuts, green olives, mayonnaise

Use Peanut Butter with:

Chopped crisp bacon, raw apple
Grated raw carrot, chopped raisins, chopped celery
Chopped dates, chopped figs, lemon juice, sliced or mashed bananas
Deviled ham, chopped dill pickles, mayonnaise
Any kind of fruit preserves

Use Softened Cream Cheese with:

Chopped cooked dried prunes, apricots
Chopped crisp bacon, pickle relish
Dried beef, minced onion, chili sauce
Chopped dates or figs, peanuts
Chopped green pepper, olives, celery
Finely chopped peanuts, minced onion, mayonnaise
Grated cucumbers

Cheese Dip

2 cups shredded Cheddar cheese
2 tablespoons blue cheese
¼ cup salad dressing or mayonnaise
2 tablespoons prepared mustard
2 tablespoons horseradish
3 to 4 tablespoons milk

Blend cheeses together. Add salad dressing or mayonnaise, mustard, and horseradish and beat until well blended. Add enough milk to make dip the right consistency. Yield: about 1½ cups.

Chili-Cheese Dip

1 (2-pound) loaf processed American cheese
2 medium onions, chopped
2 tablespoons butter or margarine
2 (15½-ounce) cans chili without beans
  Chili powder to taste
  Dash Tabasco sauce

Melt cheese in top of double boiler. Brown chopped onions in butter or margarine; add to cheese with other ingredients. Blend well. Serve hot. Yield: 4 pints.

Avocado Dip

  ¾ cup sieved avocado
  1 clove garlic
  1½ teaspoons freshly squeezed
     lemon juice
  3 tablespoons minced parsley
  ¾ teaspoon celery seed
  ¼ teaspoon salt
     Few drops Tabasco sauce
  1 teaspoon grated onion
  ½ teaspoon prepared mustard

Cut avocado into halves and remove seed and skin. Force fruit through a sieve. Rub bowl with cut garlic and discard garlic. Add avocado and other ingredients, blend well. Chill. Yield: 1 cup.

Green Dragon Dip

  1 ripe avocado
  1 (3-ounce) package cream cheese
  3 tablespoons mayonnaise or
     salad dressing
     Few drops freshly squeezed lemon
     juice or vinegar
  ¼ teaspoon seasoned salt
  ⅛ teaspoon pepper
     Grated onion (optional)

Peel, pit, and mash avocado. Mix with remaining ingredients and blend well. Add grated onion, if desired. Chill before serving. Yield: 1 cup.

Double-Ring Sandwiches

  2 hard-cooked eggs, chopped
  ⅓ cup chopped, cooked bacon
  3 tablespoons mayonnaise or
     salad dressing
  3 slices whole wheat bread
  3 slices white bread
  1 tablespoon soft butter or margarine
  12 slices stuffed green olives

Combine eggs, bacon, and mayonnaise or salad dressing. Cut each slice of bread into two 2-inch rounds, then cut the center from half of the rounds to form circles. Spread butter or margarine on rounds, then spread with 1 tablespoon egg-bacon filling. Place a circle of bread over filling, and place a slice of stuffed olive in the center of each circle. Yield: 12 party sandwiches.

Deviled Ham Dip

  2 (3-ounce) cans deviled ham
  1 cup commercial sour cream
  2 teaspoons chopped capers (optional)
  1½ tablespoons chopped pimiento
  ⅛ teaspoon black pepper
     Few drops Tabasco sauce

Combine all ingredients. Chill before serving. Yield: 2 cups.

Party Dip

  2 tablespoons butter or margarine
  3 tablespoons all-purpose flour
  ½ teaspoon salt
  1 cup milk
  ½ cup shredded Cheddar cheese
  ½ cup mayonnaise or salad dressing
  ¼ cup catsup
  ¼ teaspoon Worcestershire sauce

Melt butter or margarine in top of double boiler. Blend in flour and salt. Slowly add milk, stirring constantly. Blend in cheese, mayonnaise or salad dressing, catsup, and Worcestershire sauce and cook until cheese melts and sauce thickens. Yield: 2 cups.

Cheese Straws

  1 pound American cheese
  ¼ pound butter or margarine
  2 cups self-rising flour
  ⅛ teaspoon red pepper

Grind cheese, mix with butter or margarine, and stir well. Add flour and red pepper and mix well. Make into a roll and put in cookie press. Bake on greased cookie sheets at 400° for 8 to 10 minutes. Yield: 3 dozen.

Pimiento Cheese Sandwich Filling

1 (5⅓-ounce) can evaporated milk
½ pound processed American cheese, diced
1 (3-ounce) can pimientos
¼ teaspoon salt
  Pickles (optional)
  Chopped olives (optional)
  Grated onion (optional)

Put milk into top of double boiler. Add diced cheese, and keep hot until melted. Drain pimientos and mash. Add to cheese and milk with the salt. Pickles, chopped olives, or grated onion may be added, if desired. Yield: 1¾ cups or filling for 10 sandwiches.

Cheese Ball

2½ pounds cream cheese
2½ pounds American cheese, shredded
¼ pound blue cheese
2 tablespoons Worcestershire sauce
½ cup mayonnaise
10 drops Tabasco sauce
  Onion salt and garlic salt to taste
  Chopped walnuts

Thoroughly mix all ingredients except walnuts. Shape into balls and roll in chopped walnuts. Chill until firm and ready to serve. Yield: 3 cheese balls.

Sloppy Joes

1 pound ground beef
½ cup chopped celery
½ cup chopped onion
¼ cup chopped green pepper
1 clove garlic, minced (optional)
2 cups canned tomatoes
2 teaspoons salt
¼ teaspoon chili powder
1 teaspoon Worcestershire sauce
  Hamburger buns

Brown meat in heavy skillet; add celery, onion, green pepper, and garlic; cook for 5 minutes. Add the tomatoes and seasonings. Cover and simmer for 30 minutes. Serve over split toasted hamburger buns. Yield: 4 to 6 servings.

Chicken Salad Tea Sandwiches

⅔ cup chopped, cooked chicken
¼ cup chopped celery
⅛ teaspoon salt
3 tablespoons mayonnaise or salad dressing
2 tablespoons chopped green olives
4 slices thin-sliced sandwich bread
4 teaspoons soft butter or margarine

Combine chicken, celery, salt, mayonnaise or salad dressing, and olives. Spread each slice of bread with 1 teaspoon butter or margarine, then with 3 tablespoons chicken salad mixture. Trim crusts and cut each slice crosswise into four finger sandwiches. Yield: 16 open-face finger sandwiches.

Popcorn Balls

5 quarts popped popcorn
2 cups sugar
½ cup white corn syrup
⅓ teaspoon salt
1½ cups water
1 tablespoon vanilla extract

Discard any grains of the corn that are not tender, and put the perfect kernels in a large pan. Combine sugar, corn syrup, salt, and water in a saucepan, stir until well mixed, and then bring to boil. Boil without stirring to 260° or until candy threads from the spoon. Add vanilla. Remove from heat and pour slowly over corn, stirring and turning it with a spoon so every kernel will be coated with syrup. Make the sugared corn into balls and wrap in waxed paper. Yield: about 20 balls.

Party Mix

⅔ cup butter or margarine
1 tablespoon Worcestershire sauce
¼ teaspoon salt
⅛ teaspoon garlic salt or powder
2 cups bite-sized shredded wheat
2 cups bite-sized shredded rice
2 cups salted peanuts
   Pretzel sticks

Melt butter or margarine in shallow pan over low heat. Stir in Worcestershire sauce, salt, and garlic salt. Add other ingredients; mix gently until all pieces are covered with butter or margarine. Bake at 300° about 30 minutes, stirring gently every 10 minutes. Spread out to cool. Yield: 8 cups.

Molasses Popcorn Balls

1½ quarts popcorn (popped)
¼ teaspoon salt
½ cup light molasses
½ cup dark corn syrup
1½ teaspoons vinegar
1½ tablespoons butter or margarine

Put the popcorn into a very large bowl, and sprinkle with salt. Combine molasses, corn syrup, and vinegar in a saucepan; cook, stirring occasionally, until a drop of mixture forms a soft ball in cold water (240°). Continue cooking, stirring constantly, to 270° or until a little mixture in cold water is slightly brittle. Remove from heat, add butter or margarine, and stir only enough to mix. Pour over popcorn, tossing to coat each kernel. Shape into balls. Yield: 10 (2½-inch) popcorn balls.

Mystery Snacks

½ cup cornmeal
1 cup all-purpose flour
1 teaspoon salt
⅓ cup shortening
½ cup shredded sharp cheese
¼ cup milk

Combine cornmeal, flour, and salt. Cut in shortening and cheese until mixture resembles coarse crumbs. Add milk, stirring lightly only until dry ingredients are dampened.

Knead gently for a few seconds on lightly floured board. Roll out to ⅛-inch thickness. Cut into strips, triangles, diamonds, or other fancy shapes. Place on baking sheet and bake at 375° for 12 to 15 minutes or until delicately browned. Serve warm or cold. Yield: 3 dozen.

Cheese Snacks

¼ pound butter or margarine
¼ pound sharp cheese, shredded
1 tablespoon Worcestershire sauce
1½ cups all-purpose flour
¼ teaspoon cayenne pepper
¼ teaspoon paprika
1 teaspoon salt
   Pecan halves
1 egg white, beaten

Blend butter or margarine with shredded cheese until smooth. Add the Worcestershire sauce. Combine dry ingredients and add to butter mixture. Mix thoroughly and shape into small balls. Place on ungreased cookie sheet and press with fork. Brush pecan halves with egg white; place on top of Cheese Snacks. Bake at 325° for 25 minutes. Yield: 50.

Salted Pumpkin Seeds

Remove stringy fiber that clings to pumpkin seeds. Spread seeds on a baking sheet and roast at 300° for 15 to 20 minutes. Do not brown. Melt a little butter or margarine in a skillet; add seeds and brown lightly, shaking the pan constantly. Drain on absorbent paper towels and salt lightly.

Blackberry Shrub

4 cups blackberry juice
  Sugar syrup
1 cup grape juice
  Juice of 2 lemons

Strain juice from canned blackberries, pressing through as much pulp as possible, and measure. If you use fresh berries, prepare juice by cooking berries with just enough water to keep them from burning, and strain. Sweeten to taste with sugar syrup; add grape juice, lemon juice, and chill. Fill glasses one-third full and add water or crushed ice. Yield: 1½ quarts.

Note: Fresh raspberries or loganberries, as well as canned berries, may be used.

Christmas Party Punch

1 (12-ounce) can frozen orange juice
  concentrate
1 (6-ounce) can frozen lemonade
  concentrate
1 (18-ounce) can pineapple juice
6 cups water
6 pints cranberry juice cocktail

Add water to frozen concentrates as directed on cans. Mix all ingredients well. Serve in punchbowl over ice. Yield: 50 servings.

Fruit Juice Punch

3 cups sugar
3 quarts water
1 cup strong tea
  Juice of 12 lemons
  Juice of 12 oranges
4 cups grape juice
1 (8-ounce) can crushed pineapple
8 cups ginger ale

Boil sugar and water 8 minutes. Chill; add tea, juices, and pineapple. Set in refrigerator to mellow. Just before serving, add the ginger ale. Yield: 50 servings.

Golden Punch

2 cups freshly squeezed lemon juice
6 cups orange juice
8 cups apple juice
4 cups sugar syrup, or sweeten to taste
1 quart orange sherbet (optional)

Combine all ingredients and chill. Add 1 quart orange sherbet just before serving, if desired. Yield: about 30 servings.

Hot Fruit Punch

 4 teaspoons tea leaves
 2 cups boiling water
 2 cups sugar
 2 cups orange juice
 1 cup freshly squeezed lemon juice
 1 cup pineapple juice
2½ quarts boiling water
   Orange and lemon slices

Steep tea in boiling water for 5 minutes. Strain. Add sugar to hot tea and let cool. Prepare fruit juices and keep in a glass quart jar, covered tightly, until ready to use. Then add boiling water; mix all ingredients in punchbowl and garnish with orange and lemon slices. Serve while hot. Yield: 32 small servings.

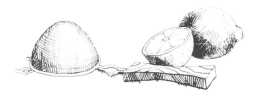

Fruit Punch

1 cup water
2 cups sugar
1 cup strong, hot tea
2 cups fruit syrup
1 cup freshly squeezed lemon juice
2 cups pineapple juice
  Ice water
1 cup maraschino cherries
4 cups ginger ale

Boil water and sugar for 5 minutes; add tea, fruit syrup, and juices. Let stand for 30 minutes; add ice water to make 1½ gallons of liquid. Add cherries and ginger ale. Serve in punchbowl with large piece of ice. Yield: 50 servings.

Citrus Punch

1½ cups sugar
 3 cups water
 1 tablespoon instant tea
1½ cups lime juice
 2 (46-ounce) cans blended grapefruit
    and orange juice
    Ice cubes
 4 cups ginger ale

Combine sugar and water in saucepan; place over low heat and stir until sugar is dissolved. Add to instant tea. Add juices; chill. Pour into punchbowl; add ice cubes; stir until ice is partially melted. Just before serving, add ginger ale. Garnish with lime slices and maraschino cherries. Yield: 44 (½-cup) servings.

Mint Punch

 1 cup powdered sugar
 4 lemons
24 sprigs of mint, chopped fine
 1 cup sugar
12 stalks mint
 8 cups ginger ale
 4 cups water
 4 cups shaved ice

Mix powdered sugar, lemon juice, and mint sprigs and set aside for 2 hours. Combine granulated sugar, mint stalks, water, and cut up rind of the 4 lemons. Boil together about 5 minutes; allow to cool. Stir the two mixtures together and strain. To 1 quart of this stock add, just before serving, 2 quarts of ginger ale, 1 quart shaved ice. Stock may be made several days ahead of use and stored in refrigerator. Yield: 1 gallon punch.

Pineapple-Lime Punch

 3 quarts unsweetened pineapple juice
    Juice of 8 lemons
    Juice of 8 oranges
    Juice of 3 limes
 2 cups sugar
 4 quarts ginger ale
 2 quarts plain soda water
    Green food coloring (optional)

Combine fruit juices and sugar. Chill thoroughly. Just before serving, add ginger ale and soda water. Tint a delicate green, if you wish. Yield: 35 cups.

Coffee Milk Shake

 1 cup strong fresh coffee
    Pinch salt
    Ice cubes
 2 large scoops vanilla ice cream
1½ tablespoons sugar
    Whipped cream
    Shaved chocolate

Pour hot coffee over ice cubes to cool. Then put coffee, salt, ice cream, and sugar into mixing bowl. Beat just long enough to blend. Serve in a tall glass. Garnish with whipped cream and shaved chocolate. Yield: 1 serving.

Hot Cider

 1 gallon sweet cider
    Juice of 4 oranges
    Juice of 5 lemons
 2 cups sugar
½ teaspoon ground nutmeg
 3 teaspoons ground allspice
 1 teaspoon ground cinnamon
 4 sticks cinnamon

Mix cider, orange juice, lemon juice, and sugar in saucepan. Tie nutmeg, allspice, and ground cinnamon in a cheesecloth bag. Add to liquid, and let boil. Remove spice bag and then float cinnamon sticks on top. Serve hot. Yield: 30 servings.

Mulled Cider

  8 cups apple cider
  ½ cup brown sugar, firmly packed
12 whole cloves
  2 (2-inch) cinnamon sticks

Combine all ingredients in a saucepan.
Bring to a boil; simmer for 5 minutes.
Strain and serve hot in mugs or cups.
Yield: 12 servings.

Tomato Juice Cocktail

  1 quart canned tomato juice
  1 teaspoon sugar
    Juice of 1 lemon
  ½ cup kraut juice
  ¼ teaspoon grated horseradish or ½
    teaspoon chili sauce
    Salt and pepper to taste

Mix ingredients together. Chill and
serve. Yield: 8 (4-ounce) servings.

Eggnog

4 eggs
4 tablespoons honey
  Pinch salt
3 cups whole milk

Beat eggs until thick and lemon colored.
Add honey, salt, and milk and mix well.
Serve cold. Yield: 4 servings.

Fruit Milk Shake

  1 or 2 bananas
  ½ cup orange juice
  ¼ cup freshly squeezed lemon juice
  1 cup canned pineapple juice
  4 cups milk (use whole milk or 2 cups
    evaporated milk and 2 cups water)

Mash bananas, and add fruit juices.
Chill thoroughly and pour into cold
milk. Beat with egg beater. Serve cold.
Yield: 4 servings.

Spiced Lemonade

  ¾ cup sugar
  ¾ cup water
12 whole cloves
  1 (3-inch) stick cinnamon
  6 lemons
  4 cups water
    Decorated ice cubes

Boil sugar and ¾ cup water about 5
minutes. Combine 1 cup of the syrup
with spices and cook 5 minutes. Strain.
Add juice of lemons and quart of water.
Chill. Pour over ice cubes when ready to
serve. Lemon-decorated ice cubes or
cubes with whole cloves frozen in them
will add appeal to this summertime
favorite. Yield: 6 servings.

Hot Spiced Tea

1 cup sugar
1 cup water
2 sticks cinnamon
½ cup orange juice
½ cup pineapple juice
¼ cup freshly squeezed lemon juice
6 cups water
6 tea bags or 6 tablespoons tea

Combine sugar, water, and cinnamon,
and boil for 5 minutes. Add fruit juices
and tea made by steeping tea bags in hot
water 5 minutes. Grated rind may be
added, if desired. For a mild cinnamon
flavor, remove sticks from syrup before
adding juices and tea. Serve piping hot.
Yield: 10 to 12 servings.

Hot Tea

1 cup boiling water
1 teaspoon tea
½ teaspoon sugar
  Lemon or cream

Pour briskly boiling water over tea,
cover, and steep 3 to 5 minutes. Strain,
and add sugar and sliced lemon or a
small amount of cream. Yield: 1 serving.

Grape Juice-Lime Cooler

¼ cup chilled grape juice
 1 tablespoon sugar or corn syrup
 2 tablespoons chilled milk
   Carbonated water

In each glass, blend grape juice and sugar or corn syrup. Slowly stir in chilled milk. Add carbonated water to fill glasses within 1½ inches of top. Top with a scoop of frozen lime sherbet, and serve at once. Yield: 1 (8-ounce) glass.

Orangenog

1½ cups chilled orange juice
 1 tablespoon freshly squeezed
   lemon juice
 3 tablespoons sugar
 2 cups chilled milk

Mix first three ingredients and stir slowly into milk. For egg-orangenog: Add fruit juice mixture gradually to 2 well beaten eggs, then stir into diluted milk and mix as directed for orangenog. Yield: 4 servings.

Peanut Butter Milk

1½ cups nonfat dry milk solids
 2 tablespoons sugar
 6 cups cold water
 ⅓ cup peanut butter

Combine milk solids and sugar; add cold water, and shake or beat until smooth. Add a small amount of mixture to peanut butter and mix until smooth. Continue adding milk until all the mixture is used. Chill thoroughly. Yield: 6 servings.

Hot Spiced Milk

1 cup milk
1 tablespoon molasses
  Dash ground cinnamon
  Ground allspice or nutmeg

Combine milk, molasses, and spices. Heat thoroughly. Pour into cup and dust with additional spices. Omit additional spices and use a stick of cinnamon for stirring, if desired. Yield: 1 serving.

Instant Spiced Tea Mix

½ cup instant tea
 2 cups orange-flavored instant
   breakfast drink
 1 (3-ounce) package sweetened
   lemonade mix
 1 teaspoon ground cloves (optional)
 1 teaspoon ground cinnamon (optional)
 2 cups sugar

Combine ingredients in large bowl and mix well. Spoon into jars and seal. To serve, add 2 teaspoons to a cup of boiling water. Yield: about 40 cups.

Hot Chocolate (or Cocoa)

4 tablespoons cocoa
4 tablespoons sugar
⅛ teaspoon salt
4 cups milk

Blend cocoa, sugar, and salt, and make syrup by using a part of the milk. Add syrup to remaining milk and heat to just below the boiling point. Serve hot, with a dash of cinnamon, or a marshmallow in each cup. Yield: 4 servings.

Beef Stew

2 tablespoons shortening
1 pound boneless beef, cut into
  1½-inch cubes
1 onion, chopped
1 medium turnip, diced
1 cup canned tomatoes
¼ cup catsup
1½ teaspoons salt
¼ teaspoon pepper
3 cups broth, or 3 beef bouillon cubes
  dissolved in 3 cups hot water
2 cups cubed, peeled potatoes
2 cups sliced, peeled carrots
6 small whole onions, peeled

Heat shortening in heavy kettle. Brown meat cubes on all sides in shortening. Add chopped onion, turnip, tomatoes, catsup, seasonings, and broth. Cover, bring to a boil; reduce heat, and simmer until meat is tender, about 1½ hours. Add vegetables and more water just to cover, if necessary. Cover and simmer until vegetables are tender. Add more salt and pepper to taste. Yield: 6 servings.

Beef Stew with Dumplings

1½ pounds lean beef (boned chuck,
  round, flank, or rump)
1½ teaspoons salt
⅛ teaspoon pepper
3 tablespoons all-purpose flour
3 tablespoons shortening
4 cups water
½ teaspoon Tabasco sauce
12 small white onions, peeled
6 medium carrots, scraped and
  quartered
1½ cups all-purpose flour
2 teaspoons baking powder
¾ teaspoon salt
¾ cup milk

Cut beef into 1½-inch pieces. Blend together ½ teaspoon of the salt, pepper, and flour. Roll pieces of meat in blended mixture. Put shortening in a heavy kettle; add beef, and brown on all sides.

Add water, ½ teaspoon of the salt, and Tabasco sauce. Cover; simmer for 2 to 2½ hours until meat is almost tender. Add remaining ½ teaspoon salt, onions, and carrots; cover, and cook until vegetables are tender. For dumplings, sift together flour, baking powder, and salt. Add milk; stir only until blended. Drop by spoonfuls on top of piece of meat or vegetable in stew. Cook uncovered for 10 minutes; cover tightly, and cook over low heat for 10 minutes longer. Yield: 6 servings.

Southern Hash

4 or 5 raw potatoes
2 medium onions
4 tablespoons shortening
½ cup tomatoes
1 cup meat stock or gravy
2 cups cooked, chopped meat
  Salt
  Pepper

Put potatoes and onions through a food chopper. Melt shortening, add potatoes, onions, and tomatoes, cover pan, and cook until potatoes are done. Stir occasionally to prevent sticking. Add chopped meat and season with salt and pepper. Heat thoroughly and serve hot. Yield: 6 servings.

Oven-Cooked Beef Stew

1 pound beef stew meat
  Salt, pepper, all-purpose flour
3 tablespoons shortening
2 medium onions, chopped
1¾ cups water
1 (10½-ounce) can condensed
  tomato soup
1 small bay leaf
2 whole cloves
1 stalk celery, sliced
4 carrots, sliced
1 cup canned peas
3 medium potatoes, cut into eighths
  Salt and pepper

Cut meat into 1-inch cubes; sprinkle with salt and pepper, and dredge with flour. Melt shortening in skillet and brown meat thoroughly. Transfer meat to a 2-quart casserole. Lightly brown chopped onions in the hot shortening; add to meat. Heat water with tomato soup and pour over meat. Add seasonings and sliced celery. Cover and bake at 325° for 1½ hours, or until meat is nearly tender. Add sliced carrots, peas, and potatoes cut in eighths; sprinkle with salt and pepper, and mix in with beef and gravy. Cover and continue baking for 45 minutes. Yield: 4 to 6 servings.

Louisiana Bouillabaisse

2½ pounds firm-fleshed fish (black bass, gaspergou), or whole pan fish (perch or bream, etc.)
     Salt and pepper
 1 cup chopped onions
 ½ cup chopped onion tops
 2 tablespoons finely cut garlic
 1 cup chopped celery
 ¼ cup chopped parsley
1¼ cups cooked tomatoes
 2 tablespoons freshly squeezed lemon juice
 2 tablespoons Worcestershire sauce
 2 tablespoons all-purpose flour
1½ pounds cleaned shrimp
 1 pound crabmeat

Bone fish and cut into serving-size pieces. Season with salt and pepper. Prepare the onions, garlic, celery, and parsley, and mix together thoroughly. Pour off some of the juice from the tomatoes and add lemon juice and Worcestershire sauce. Mix well. Add flour gradually to tomato juice mixture and make into a thin paste.

Brush olive oil or salad oil on bottom and sides of pot. A black iron pot with heavy lid is ideal for this, but an electric skillet can be used.

Place a layer of seasoned fish in the pot. Spoon the flour-tomato mixture over all

the fish. Put a layer of vegetable seasoning next. Mash a few tomatoes and sprinkle over vegetables. Put a second layer of fish, the vegetable mixture, and tomatoes until all the fish and vegetable mixture is used up. Size of the pot will determine the layers. It is possible there will be only one layer.

Place lid on pot and cook over medium heat until juice starts to boil, then reduce immediately to low heat.

Cook, covered, for 45 minutes to 1 hour, or until fish flakes easily with fork. With an electric skillet, start fish at 350°. As soon as it starts to boil, reduce to 225°; cook for 45 minutes to 1 hour, or until done. Ten minutes before stew is done, add shrimp and crabmeat. Yield: 8 to 10 servings.

Brunswick Stew No. 1

 1 (4- to 5-pound) hen
 2 pounds boneless stew meat
 1 pound onions
 3 pounds potatoes
 2 (16-ounce) cans tomatoes
 2 (17-ounce) cans cream-style corn
 1 (17-ounce) can green peas
 1 (17-ounce) can lima beans
1½ bottles catsup
 1 (14-ounce) bottle Worcestershire sauce
 ½ cup vinegar
 ¾ cup freshly squeezed lemon juice
 4 teaspoons Tabasco sauce
 2 teaspoons salt
     Black pepper

Put hen and stew meat in a saucepan with water to cover. Cook until well done or meat leaves the bone. Grind and set meat aside. Put onions and potatoes through food grinder and add to the broth. Cook until well done. Add meat and other ingredients. Cook over low heat until well done and thick (about 2 to 3 hours). Serve hot; or cool, pour into containers, and freeze. Yield: 5 to 6 quarts.

Brunswick Stew No. 2

3 squirrels, or 2 rabbits
5 quarts boiling water
1 pound salt pork, cut into strips
1 large onion, minced
4 cups chopped tomatoes
2 cups green lima beans
2 cups corn
8 to 12 diced potatoes
1 tablespoon salt
1 teaspoon black pepper
⅛ teaspoon cayenne pepper
4 teaspoons sugar
½ cup butter or margarine
4 tablespoons all-purpose flour

Cut squirrels or rabbits into serving-size pieces. Drop pieces into boiling water in a large kettle; add salt pork and minced onion. Cover and simmer for 2 hours, removing film at beginning of cooking. Add vegetables and seasonings and bring to a boil; cover and simmer 1 hour longer, stirring occasionally to prevent burning. Make a paste of butter or margarine and flour; shape into small balls and drop into stew. Boil for 10 minutes, stirring to make a smooth stew. Add more seasoning, if necessary. Yield: 12 servings.

Chicken and Oyster Gumbo

12 cups water
1 (3- to 5-pound) chicken
⅓ cup shortening
½ cup all-purpose flour
1 large onion, chopped
  Salt, black and red pepper
½ cup chopped green onion tops
⅓ cup chopped parsley
3 dozen oysters
1 tablespoon filé
  Cooked rice

Pour water into large pot. Cut chicken into serving-size pieces, and brown in hot shortening. When brown, put in pot with water; add flour to the shortening, and brown very slowly. Add onion. Let cook until slightly brown and clear; add to chicken and seasonings. Cook very slowly until chicken is tender, stirring often. Add green onion tops and parsley. Cook for 10 minutes; add oysters; let cook until oysters curl. Remove from heat, add filé, and stir; serve at once. To serve, place a serving of cooked rice in soup plate, add a piece of chicken, fill plate with gumbo. Yield: 10 to 12 servings.

Chicken Stew

1 (3- to 4-pound) stewing chicken
  Salt and pepper
½ cup shortening
3 tablespoons all-purpose flour
2 cups chopped onions
½ cup chopped celery
½ cup chopped green peppers
2 cups water
1 (4-ounce) can mushrooms
¼ cup chopped onion tops or shallots
2 tablespoons chopped parsley
  Cooked rice

Disjoint chicken; salt and pepper the pieces. Brown quickly in the shortening, and remove chicken after browning. Add flour to shortening and brown. Add onions, celery, and peppers; cook slowly until tender. Return chicken to pan. Add water and mushrooms. Cover, and simmer for about 2½ to 3 hours. Add onion tops or shallots about 10 minutes before done. Add parsley 5 minutes before removing from heat. Serve with cooked rice. Yield: 8 servings.

Grits-Beef Stew

2½ pounds beef for stew
 1 cup all-purpose flour
 2 tablespoons salt
 ½ teaspoon pepper
 6 tablespoons shortening
 2 cloves garlic, minced
 4 cups boiling water
 3 cups cooked tomatoes
 1 teaspoon Worcestershire sauce
18 small white onions, peeled and
    quartered
 7 carrots, peeled and cut into
    2-inch strips
 2 cups cooked green peas
 1 cup uncooked grits

Cut meat into 1½-inch cubes. Combine flour, salt, and pepper; coat meat well with this mixture. Melt shortening in Dutch oven; add meat and brown. Add garlic, boiling water, tomatoes, and Worcestershire sauce. Cover and simmer for about 2 hours or until meat is tender. Add onions and carrots, and cook an additional 20 minutes. Add more salt, if needed. Add peas and uncooked grits; cook for 15 minutes. Yield: 8 servings.

Country-Style Chicken Soup

 1 (4-pound) stewing chicken,
    cut into pieces
 1 cup chopped onion
 1 carrot, peeled and quartered
 1 bay leaf
 1 teaspoon salt
 8 cups water
 ½ cup fresh breadcrumbs
 ½ teaspoon salt
 ½ teaspoon poultry seasoning
 1 egg
 1 tablespoon chopped parsley
 2 carrots, peeled
 2 stalks celery
 ¼ cup chicken fat
 ⅓ cup all-purpose flour
 1 cup milk

Place chicken in a large heavy pot with onion, quartered carrot, bay leaf, 1 teaspoon salt, and water; simmer for 2 to 3 hours, or until tender; remove chicken and chill stock. Remove chicken from bones; discard skin; reserve 1 cup chicken for soup. (Chill remainder to use for salad, casserole, or other chicken dish.) Grind 1 cup chicken; add breadcrumbs, ½ teaspoon salt, poultry seasoning, egg, and parsley; blend. Form firmly into small balls; set aside. Remove layer of fat from chilled stock; reserve. Heat chicken stock (there should be 4 cups). Cut carrots and celery into matchstick-size pieces; add to stock; cook for 10 to 15 minutes, or until tender. Melt ¼ cup chicken fat in saucepan; blend in flour; add milk slowly, stirring constantly. Pour mixture slowly into stock; cook, stirring constantly, until mixture is thickened. Drop chicken balls into soup; heat for 5 minutes more; serve. Yield: 4 to 6 servings.

Okra-Shrimp Gumbo

 1 thin slice ham
 4 cups okra, sliced thin
 2 cups chopped onions
 2 cloves garlic, chopped
 3 teaspoons chopped parsley
 1 (8-ounce) can tomato sauce
 2 pounds fresh shrimp
 4 cups water
 1 teaspoon seafood seasoning (optional)
 ½ teaspoon red pepper
 1 teaspoon salt
 ½ teaspoon pepper
    Cooked rice

Cut ham into small pieces. Sauté lightly in a skillet. Add okra, and brown lightly, stirring constantly. Add onions, garlic, parsley, and tomato sauce, and let simmer for a few minutes. Add shrimp, water, seafood seasoning, red pepper, salt, and pepper. Let cook for 1 hour over very slow heat. Serve over cooked rice. Yield: 6 to 8 servings.

Pine Bark Fish Stew

    6 slices bacon
    6 medium onions, chopped
 2½   cups canned tomatoes
    3 pounds fish
       Salt
       Black and red pepper
    1 (6-ounce) can tomato paste
    4 cups water
    3 tablespoons butter or margarine
    1 teaspoon Worcestershire sauce
    1 cup catsup

Fry bacon until crisp. Remove from pan. Fry onions slowly in bacon drippings until brown. Add sieved tomatoes to tomato paste and let boil until tomatoes are thoroughly cooked (about 5 minutes). Add onions, bacon drippings, water, and butter or margarine. Boil for 10 minutes. Drop in fish which has been cut into eight pieces; season well with salt, black and red pepper, Worcestershire sauce, and catsup. Boil slowly until the fish is tender, then break bacon into small pieces and drop into stew. Yield: 6 to 8 servings.

New Year's Eve Oyster Stew

    5 tablespoons butter
    3 dozen oysters, shucked and
       with liquid
    2 tablespoons Worcestershire sauce
    1 teaspoon salt
   ¼ teaspoon seasoned pepper
    6 cups whole milk or half milk and
       half cream
   ½ bunch parsley, minced
       Paprika to taste
       Butter

Heat the butter in a deep, heavy kettle. When it bubbles, add oysters, Worcestershire sauce, salt, and seasoned pepper. Cook gently until the edges of the oysters begin to curl (about a minute). Heat the milk until hot but not boiling; combine with the oysters and simmer briefly but do not boil. Let stand

to blend the flavors. When ready to serve, heat until hot but not boiling. Pour into a warm tureen and top with minced parsley, paprika to taste, and dots of butter. Yield: 8 servings.

Fresh Vegetable and Chicken Stew

    1 (4- to 5-pound) chicken
    2 to 3 tablespoons shortening
    2 cups hot water
    1 tablespoon salt
   ¾ teaspoon black pepper
   12 small white onions
    1 cup sliced carrots
    1 cup fresh peas, lima beans, or
       snap beans
    1 cup diced potatoes
   ⅓ cup all-purpose flour
   ½ cup water

Cut chicken into serving-size pieces and brown on all sides in hot shortening. Place in Dutch oven or saucepan with water, salt, and pepper. Cover and cook for 1 hour, or until chicken is tender. Add vegetables about 30 minutes before cooking time is up. Combine flour with the ½ cup water and stir into stew. Cook until medium thickness. Yield: 6 servings.

Irish Stew

    2 pounds boned shoulder of lamb, cut
       into 2-inch pieces
    4 cups water
    2 sprigs parsley
    1 bay leaf
    2 celery tops
    2 teaspoons salt
    2 cups cubed rutabagas
    3 medium potatoes, peeled and halved
    6 small onions, peeled
    2 tablespoons all-purpose flour
    3 tablespoons water

Put lamb into saucepan with water,

parsley, bay leaf, celery tops, and salt. Cover; simmer for 1½ hours, or until lamb is tender. Add cubed rutabagas, halved potatoes, and onions; cover, and cook until vegetables are tender. Then set aside and make a smooth paste of flour and water. Gradually add to stew, stirring constantly until thickened. Yield: 6 servings.

Beef Brisket Soup

    2 pounds beef brisket
    8 cups water
    1 tablespoon salt
    5 medium potatoes, peeled and diced
      Dash celery salt
    1 large onion, chopped
    ½ cup shredded American or
      Cheddar cheese
    ⅔ cup oatmeal
    1 (1-pound) can cream-style
      corn (optional)

Cut brisket into pieces; simmer, covered, in salted water. When meat is tender, add potatoes, celery salt, onion, cheese, and oatmeal. Add corn, if desired. Continue to cook, covered, until vegetables are done, stirring once or twice while cooking. Remove from heat and serve in separate small bowls, allowing a piece of beef for each bowl. Yield: 8 servings.

Southern Corn Chowder

    ½ pound bacon, cut into 1-inch pieces
    2 small onions, sliced
    1 tablespoon all-purpose flour
    1 cup water
    2 cups finely diced raw potatoes
    ½ cup chopped celery
    2 bay leaves
    2 (1-pound) cans cream-style corn
    1 cup milk
    1 teaspoon salt
    ¼ teaspoon white pepper

Fry bacon until crisp, drain on absorbent

paper, and set aside. Reserve ¼ cup bacon drippings and place in a kettle. Sauté onion in bacon drippings for about 5 minutes. Blend in flour and mix to a smooth paste. Gradually add the water and stir until smooth. Add the potatoes, celery, and bay leaves. Cover and cook over low heat for about 15 minutes or until potatoes are done. Stir occasionally. Blend in corn, milk, seasonings, and bacon. Heat for 15 minutes. Serve hot. Yield: 5 to 6 servings.

Maryland Clam Chowder

    12 cups water
    1 whole chicken breast
    3 tablespoons chicken stock base
    1 teaspoon salt
    2 stalks celery, with tops
    1 tablespoon freeze-dried
      chopped chives
    2 tablespoons minced onion
    ½ teaspoon celery salt
    ¼ teaspoon thyme leaves
    ¼ teaspoon white pepper
    1 cup sliced carrots
    1 cup diced potatoes
    1 (10-ounce) package frozen corn
    1 (10-ounce) package frozen peas
    1 whole pimiento, chopped fine
    1 cup clam juice
    1 teaspoon parsley flakes
 1½ cups minced Chesapeake Bay
      soft-shell clams (about 3 dozen)

Combine water, chicken, chicken stock base, salt, and celery in a large saucepan; simmer for 1 hour. Discard celery, remove chicken, and finely chop the meat; set aside. To the stock add remaining ingredients except the clam juice, parsley flakes, clams, and chopped chicken. Simmer for 20 minutes; then add remaining ingredients. Continue cooking for 5 minutes. Yield: 4 quarts.

Kentucky Burgoo

2 pounds foreshank soup bone
2 pounds pork shank
2 pounds veal shank
1 (3- to 5-pound) breast of lamb
1 (5- to 6-pound) hen
8 quarts cold water
3 large onions, chopped
3 large potatoes, chopped
3 raw carrots, chopped
1 cup diced celery
4 cups tomatoes, chopped
2 cups corn
2 cups butterbeans
2 pods red pepper
2 green peppers, chopped
  Salt and cayenne pepper to taste
4 teaspoons Worcestershire sauce
  Small bunch parsley, finely chopped

Put the soup bone and all the meat
into cold water in a 4-gallon kettle,
and bring slowly to a boil. Simmer until
meat is tender enough to fall from the
bones. Lift meat out of stock; cool; remove from bones; chop. Add onions,
potatoes, carrots, celery, tomatoes, corn,
butterbeans, red and green peppers.
Allow to simmer until thick. Add salt
and cayenne pepper to taste.

Burgoo should be very thick, but soupy.
Stir frequently during the first part of
cooking and almost constantly after it
thickens. Test occasionally and add
more seasoning if necessary. Total cooking time should be about 10 hours. Add
Worcestershire sauce 10 minutes before
removing from heat. Add chopped parsley just before serving. Yield: 10
quarts.

Meatball Chowder

½ cup breadcrumbs
½ cup milk
1 pound beef
½ pound pork
½ pound veal
1 cup diced raw potatoes
½ cup diced celery
1 egg
1 teaspoon salt
⅛ teaspoon ground nutmeg
¼ cup chopped onion
¼ teaspoon pepper
¼ teaspoon brown sugar
⅛ teaspoon ground allspice
2 tablespoons shortening
1 (10½-ounce) can tomato soup
1 cup water
1 cup diced raw potatoes
1 cup green beans
½ cup diced celery

Soak breadcrumbs in the milk. Grind
beef, pork, veal, potatoes, and celery.
Add soaked breadcrumbs, and mix
thoroughly. Add the egg, salt, nutmeg,
onion, pepper, brown sugar, and allspice, and shape into balls no larger than
1 inch in diameter. Brown in hot shortening. Add the soup, water, raw potatoes, green beans, and celery. Simmer
until vegetables are cooked. Yield: 6
to 8 servings.

Cream of Peanut Butter Soup

6 cups peanut butter
24 cups milk
6 tablespoons all-purpose flour
  Salt and pepper to taste
6 tablespoons chopped onion

Put peanut butter into a bowl and gradually add 6 cups of cold milk to thin it.
Scald the remainder of the milk over hot
water, then mix it with the flour. Add
salt and pepper, then combine with the
peanut butter and milk mixture. Add
finely chopped onion and stir well.
Serve very hot. Yield: 24 servings.

Split-Pea Soup

    1 pound (2¼ cups) green split peas
2½ quarts water
    1 meaty ham bone
1½ cups sliced onion
  ½ teaspoon pepper
  ¼ teaspoon garlic salt
  ¼ teaspoon marjoram
    1 cup diced celery
    1 cup sliced carrots
    1 teaspoon parsley flakes
      Salt to taste

Wash peas and put into water. Soak overnight. Or, bring water to boiling point; add washed beans; boil for 2 minutes only; cover; remove from heat; allow to stand for 1 hour. (This is equal to 12 to 15 hours soaking in cold water.)

Add ham bone, onion, and seasonings. Bring to a boil; cover; and simmer for 2 hours; stirring occasionally. Remove bone; cut off any bits of meat. Return meat to soup; add remaining ingredients. Cook slowly for 45 minutes. Serve with oyster crackers. Yield: 8 to 10 servings.

Farm-Style Onion Soup

    4 cups beef stock
    1 bay leaf
      Pinch thyme
      Salt and pepper
  ¼ pound butter or margarine
    1 clove garlic, minced
    2 cups thinly sliced onions
      Toast squares
      Shredded cheese

Combine beef stock, bay leaf, thyme, salt, and pepper, and bring to a boil. Check flavor, and add more seasoning if desired. Melt butter or margarine in a deep skillet or Dutch oven. Add garlic, and simmer until garlic is browned, then discard garlic. Add onions; cover and simmer over low heat until onions are just soft and transparent. Mix the onions and hot stock. To serve, place toast squares in bottom of soup bowl, sprinkle with shredded cheese, and pour soup over them. Yield: 6 cups.

Okra Soup

    2 pounds lean beef, cut into cubes
    1 onion, sliced
    4 tablespoons shortening
  12 cups water
      Salt
      Pepper
    2 cups sliced okra
  ½ cup uncooked regular rice
    1 cup sliced tomatoes

Brown cubed beef and sliced onion in hot shortening. Add water, and salt and pepper to taste. Let cook slowly until beef is tender. Add sliced okra, rice, and sliced tomatoes. Let cook until beef is very tender and vegetables are cooked. Yield: 8 servings.

Black-Eyed Pea Soup

    1 cup dried black-eyed peas
    2 cups boiling water
    4 cups cold water
  ¾ teaspoon salt
      Pepper to taste
    6 slices bacon
      Lemon slices
  ½ cup cream, whipped (optional)
      Ground nutmeg (optional)

Wash peas. Pour boiling water over them and soak for 6 hours or overnight. Add the cold water, salt, pepper, and 1 slice bacon. Bring to a boil, cover, and simmer for 2 hours. Mash peas to a smooth paste (a blender is fine for this), and heat with the liquid to the boiling point. Cook 5 slices of bacon until crisp, and crumble in the bottom of soup bowls. Add a very thin slice of lemon to each bowl. Fill bowls with soup, float a spoonful of whipped cream on top of each and sprinkle with nutmeg. Yield: 6 to 8 servings.

Bing Cherry Salad

1 (17-ounce) can pitted bing
  cherries, drained
3 (3-ounce) packages
  cherry-flavored gelatin
1 envelope unflavored gelatin
½ cup cold water
3 (3-ounce) packages cream
  cheese, softened
1 (20-ounce) can crushed pineapple
2 (6-ounce) bottles cola beverage
  Chopped nuts (optional)

Heat cherry juice and dissolve cherry
gelatin in this. Add unflavored gelatin
to ½ cup cold water; add to hot gelatin
mixture and stir until dissolved. Mash
cream cheese and add to warm mixture.
Add 1 cup each of cherries and un-
drained pineapple. Chill slightly. Add
remainder of cherries and pineapple.
Add cola beverage, and nuts, if desired.
Chill in refrigerator until firm. Yield:
6 to 8 servings.

Creamy Frozen Fruit Salad

¼ cup sugar
½ teaspoon salt
1½ tablespoons all-purpose flour
¾ cup syrup drained from fruit
1 egg, slightly beaten
2 tablespoons vinegar
1 cup drained, diced canned pears
¾ cup drained pineapple tidbits
2 cups mashed, medium-ripe bananas
½ cup drained, chopped,
  maraschino cherries
1 cup chopped pecans
⅔ cup evaporated milk
1 tablespoon freshly squeezed
  lemon juice

Combine sugar, salt, and flour in saucepan. Add fruit syrup, egg, and vinegar.
Cook over medium heat, stirring constantly until thickened. Cool. Add fruit
and nuts to cooled mixture. Chill evaporated milk in freezer until soft ice
crystals form (about 10 or 15 minutes). Whip until stiff, about 1 minute.

Add lemon juice; whip for 1 additional
minute to make very stiff. Fold into
fruit mixture. Spoon into lightly oiled
6½-cup mold. Freeze until firm, about
5 to 6 hours. Yield: 12 servings.

Creamy Fruit Salad

1 (3-ounce) package lemon-
  flavored gelatin
¾ cup hot fruit cocktail syrup
1 cup cottage cheese
1⅓ cups drained, canned fruit cocktail
½ cup chopped nuts
½ cup chopped, unpeeled apples
¼ cup freshly squeezed lemon juice
1 cup undiluted evaporated milk

Dissolve gelatin in hot fruit cocktail
syrup. Cool slightly. Fold in remaining
ingredients and mix well. Chill in refrigerator until firm. Yield: 6 to 8
servings.

Bing Cherry Delight Salad

1 (17-ounce) can pitted bing
  cherries, drained
1 (20-ounce) can crushed
  pineapple, drained
3 (3-ounce) packages cherry-
  flavored gelatin
1½ cups boiling water
1½ cups boiling pineapple juice
1½ cups boiling cherry juice
⅔ cup freshly squeezed lemon juice
½ envelope unflavored gelatin
⅔ cup ice water

Drain cherries and pineapple. Dissolve
fruit-flavored gelatin in boiling water
and juices. Dissolve unflavored gelatin
in ice water and add to boiling mixture.
Stir to dissolve. Let chill to consistency
of unbeaten egg white. Add cherries
and pineapple just before it congeals.
Yield: 6 to 8 servings.

Cranberry Salad

2 cups sugar
1 cup water
2½ tablespoons unflavored gelatin
½ cup cold water
4 cups raw cranberries, ground
1 medium orange with rind, ground
1 cup chopped celery
1 cup chopped nuts

Cook sugar and 1 cup water to make a thin syrup. Add gelatin which has been soaked in ½ cup cold water; stir until dissolved; cool. Add other ingredients; pour into an 8-cup mold and chill. Yield: 8 to 10 servings.

Orange Sherbet Salad

2 (3-ounce) packages orange-flavored gelatin
1 cup boiling water
1 pint orange sherbet
1 (8¼-ounce) can crushed pineapple
1 cup miniature marshmallows
1 (11-ounce) can mandarin orange sections, drained
½ pint whipping cream, whipped

Dissolve gelatin in boiling water. Add orange sherbet. When partially set, add other ingredients, folding in the whipped cream last. Chill until firm. Yield: 12 servings.

Pineapple Salad

1 (20-ounce) can crushed pineapple, drained
1 (3-ounce) package lemon- or orange-flavored gelatin
2 (3-ounce) packages cream cheese, softened
1 cup chopped celery
1 cup chopped nuts
1 (3-ounce) can pimientos, chopped
1 cup mayonnaise or salad dressing

Measure juice drained from pineapple; add water to make 2 cups. Heat liquid to boiling and dissolve gelatin in liquid.

Add other ingredients and stir well. Spoon into a 10-cup mold or pan and chill in refrigerator. Stir mixture several times. Yield: 8 to 10 servings.

Waldorf Salad

2 cups diced apples
Juice of ½ lemon
1 cup chopped celery
½ cup chopped pecans
Mayonnaise or salad dressing
Lettuce leaves

Put diced apples into large bowl; sprinkle with lemon juice. Add celery and nuts, and toss. Add mayonnaise or salad dressing to hold together, and serve on lettuce leaves. Yield: 4 to 6 servings.

Sweet Relish Congealed Salad

1 envelope unflavored gelatin
¼ cup cold water
¾ cup boiling water
1 cup sugar
½ cup cider vinegar
1 tablespoon tarragon-flavored vinegar
1 cup sweet pickle relish
1 (8½-ounce) can crushed pineapple, drained
½ cup finely chopped pecans
Ripe stuffed olives

Sprinkle gelatin in cold water. Add to boiling water and stir until dissolved. Add sugar and vinegars, and set aside to cool. When gelatin begins to thicken, add relish, drained pineapple, and nuts. Pour into lightly oiled 8-cup mold and chill until firm. Garnish with ripe stuffed olives. Yield: 6 to 8 servings.

24-Hour Salad

    2 eggs, well beaten
    ¼ cup freshly squeezed lemon juice
    2 tablespoons sugar
       Dash salt
    3 tablespoons butter or margarine
    1 cup heavy cream, whipped
    2 cups miniature marshmallows
    2 cups diced pineapple, drained
    2 cups pitted white cherries, drained
    ½ cup diced oranges
    1 cup halved and seeded grapes
    ¼ cup chopped blanched almonds

Combine eggs, lemon juice, sugar, and salt and cook over low heat until thick. Add butter and cool. Fold cream into cooled mixture. Combine this mixture lightly with marshmallows, well drained fruits, and nuts. Chill 24 hours so the delicate flavors will blend. Yield: 12 servings.

Roast Beef Salad

    3 cups cubed, cooked beef
    ½ cup chopped dill pickles
    ½ cup chopped celery
    ⅓ cup finely chopped onion
    ⅓ cup mayonnaise or salad dressing
    1 teaspoon prepared mustard
    1 teaspoon Worcestershire sauce
    1 teaspoon salt

Combine first four ingredients. Blend mayonnaise or salad dressing with remaining ingredients. Mix lightly with meat mixture; chill. Yield: 4 to 6 servings.

Ham and Macaroni Salad

    ½ pound boiled or baked ham
    ½ cup diced Cheddar cheese
    2 cups cooked elbow macaroni
    1 cup chopped celery
    1 small onion, chopped
    ½ cup diced dill pickle
    ½ cup mayonnaise
    2 teaspoons prepared mustard

Cut ham into ½-inch cubes. Combine ham and cheese with macaroni, celery, onion, and pickle. Mix mayonnaise and mustard; add to macaroni mixture and mix well. Chill until ready to serve. Yield: 4 servings.

Chicken Salad Supreme

    2½ cups diced cooked chicken
     2 cups chopped celery
     1 cup sliced white grapes
     ½ cup slivered toasted almonds
     ½ cup finely chopped sweet pickles
     2 tablespoons minced parsley
     4 hard-cooked eggs, chopped
     1 teaspoon salt
    1½ tablespoons unflavored gelatin
     4 tablespoons water
     ½ cup hot chicken stock
     1 cup mayonnaise
     ½ cup whipping cream, whipped

Combine chicken, celery, grapes, almonds, pickles, parsley, eggs, and salt. Soak gelatin in cold water for 5 minutes and dissolve in hot chicken stock. When cold, add mayonnaise and whipped cream. Stir until thick and fold in the chicken mixture. Yield: 8 to 10 servings.

White Fruit Salad

    4 egg yolks
    1 cup milk
    1 envelope unflavored gelatin
    ¼ cup fruit juice
    4½ cups miniature marshmallows
    1 (20-ounce) can crushed
       pineapple, drained
    1 (17-ounce) can white cherries,
       drained and pitted
    ½ pound chopped blanched almonds
       Juice of 1½ lemons
    1 cup cream, whipped

Beat egg yolks; add milk and scald in top of double boiler. Dissolve gelatin in fruit juice and add to milk and egg mixture. Cool and add remaining ingredients. Let sit in refrigerator for several hours. Yield: 10 servings.

Molded Ham Salad

1 (3-ounce) package lemon-flavored gelatin
¼ teaspoon onion salt
  Dash ground cloves
1 cup boiling water
¾ cup cold water
3 tablespoons freshly squeezed lemon juice
1½ cups chopped boiled ham
1 cup small raw cauliflower flowerets
½ cup diced celery
1 tablespoon chopped pimiento

Dissolve gelatin, onion salt, and cloves in boiling water; add cold water and lemon juice. Chill until syrupy; add remaining ingredients. Put into a 1-quart mold; chill until firm. Yield: 4 to 6 servings.

Hot Turkey Salad

2 cups diced, cooked turkey
2 cups diced celery
½ cup slivered toasted almonds
½ teaspoon salt
2 teaspoons grated onion
2 tablespoons freshly squeezed lemon juice
1 cup mayonnaise
½ cup shredded American cheese
1 cup crushed potato chips

Combine turkey, celery, almonds, salt, onion, lemon juice, and mayonnaise. Toss until well mixed. Pile lightly into greased 2-quart baking dish. Sprinkle with cheese and potato chips. Bake at 450° for 10 minutes. Serve hot. Yield: 6 servings.

Ham and Celery Salad

2 cups diced, cooked ham
1 cup chopped celery
3 sweet pickles, chopped
½ green pepper, chopped
  Mayonnaise or salad dressing

Mix ham with celery, pickles, and green pepper. Add enough mayonnaise or salad dressing to moisten. Yield: 3 to 4 servings.

Shrimp-Apple Salad

1½ pounds frozen shrimp, cooked and diced
1 cup diced celery
2 cups diced apples
¼ cup freshly squeezed lemon juice
2 tablespoons salad oil
1 teaspoon salt
3 hard-cooked eggs, coarsely chopped
¼ cup mayonnaise or salad dressing
  Lettuce cups

Combine shrimp, celery, and apples. Mix together lemon juice, salad oil, and salt, and add to shrimp mixture. Chill. Just before serving, add eggs and mayonnaise or salad dressing. Serve in lettuce cups. Yield: 6 servings.

Tuna Salad

2 (7-ounce) cans tuna
4 cups shredded salad greens
4 medium tomatoes
3 hard-cooked eggs
  Salt and pepper to taste
½ cup mayonnaise
¼ cup freshly squeezed lemon juice

Arrange salad greens in bottom of large salad bowl. Cover with tuna, and flank with quartered tomatoes and slices of hard-cooked eggs. Add seasonings and drizzle lemon juice over all. Serve with mayonnaise and garnish. Yield: 6 to 8 servings.

Tuna Fish Salad

2 (7-ounce) cans tuna fish
½ cup mayonnaise or salad dressing
1 cup chopped celery
2 tablespoons chopped sweet pickles
2 tablespoons chopped onion
2 hard-cooked eggs, chopped
½ teaspoon salt
   Lettuce

Drain tuna. Break into pieces. Combine next six ingredients and mix lightly. Serve on lettuce. Yield: 6 servings.

Carrot Congealed Salad

1 (3-ounce) package lemon-
   flavored gelatin
2 cups boiling water
2 cups shredded carrots
1 cup diced celery
1 cup drained, crushed pineapple
½ cup chopped nuts

Dissolve gelatin in boiling water. Let sit in refrigerator until mixture begins to thicken. Stir in other ingredients and spoon into individual molds. Return to refrigerator to chill. Yield: 6 servings.

Carrot-Raisin Salad

2 cups grated carrots
½ cup raisins
   Mayonnaise or salad dressing
   Coconut or drained pineapple cubes
   (optional)

Combine grated carrots and raisins and add just enough salad dressing or mayonnaise to moisten. Coconut or drained pineapple cubes may also be added. Yield: 4 servings.

Cole Slaw

4 cups shredded cabbage
1 to 3 tablespoons sugar
4 tablespoons vinegar
1 tablespoon minced onion
½ teaspoon salt
⅓ cup salad oil
   Parsley and paprika for garnish

Wash, drain, and chill cabbage. Shred. Combine sugar, vinegar, onion, salt, and salad oil. Add cabbage and mix lightly. Garnish with parsley and dash of paprika. Yield: 6 servings.

Three-Day Cole Slaw

1 medium head cabbage, chopped or
   shredded
1 medium onion, chopped
1 green pepper, chopped
1 (3-ounce) can pimiento, chopped
½ cup honey
½ cup vinegar
½ cup cooking oil
2 teaspoons sugar
2 teaspoons salt

Combine chopped cabbage, onion, pepper, and pimiento. Set aside. Combine other ingredients and bring to a hard boil. Pour hot sauce over chopped vegetables and mix well. Pack into containers and cover. Let sit in refrigerator for 3 days without removing cover. Yield: 12 servings.

Perfection Salad

1 (3-ounce) package orange- or
   lemon-flavored gelatin
1 cup boiling water
1 cup cold water
1 teaspoon salt
1 tablespoon freshly squeezed lemon juice
1 cup shredded cabbage
½ cup chopped celery
½ cup shredded carrots
1 tablespoon finely minced onion

Dissolve gelatin in boiling water; add cold water, salt, and lemon juice; chill. When mixture is slightly thick, add the cabbage, celery, carrots, and onion. Pour into mold and chill until firm. Yield: 6 to 8 servings.

Deviled Potato Salad

8 hard-cooked eggs
2 tablespoons vinegar
1 tablespoon prepared horseradish
2½ tablespoons prepared mustard
1 cup mayonnaise or salad dressing
1 cup commercial sour cream
½ teaspoon celery salt
1 teaspoon salt
6 medium potatoes, cooked in jackets, peeled and cubed (4½ cups)
1 cup chopped celery
¼ cup chopped onion
2 tablespoons chopped green pepper
2 tablespoons chopped pimiento
  Tomato wedges
  Cucumber slices

Cut eggs in half and remove yolks. Mash and blend yolks with vinegar, horseradish, and mustard. Add mayonnaise, sour cream, celery salt, and salt; mix well. Chop egg whites; combine with potatoes, celery, onion, green pepper, and pimiento. Fold in egg yolk mixture; chill. Garnish with tomato wedges and cucumber slices. Yield: 6 to 8 servings.

Hot German Potato Salad

1½ tablespoons all-purpose flour
2 tablespoons sugar
2 tablespoons bacon drippings
1 teaspoon salt
¼ teaspoon ground black pepper
½ cup water
⅓ cup cider vinegar
4 teaspoons prepared mustard
3 tablespoons minced green onion
4 cups sliced, cooked potatoes
½ teaspoon celery seed
¼ cup chopped celery
2 tablespoons diced green pepper
2 tablespoons diced pimiento
4 slices crisp bacon, crumbled

Mix flour and sugar together in a skillet. Add bacon drippings, salt, pepper, water, and vinegar. Stir and cook until thickened. Add mustard and onion. Then add potatoes, celery seed, celery, green pepper, and pimiento; mix well, but lightly. Sprinkle with bacon. Serve hot. Yield: 6 to 8 servings.

Potato Salad

½ cup mayonnaise or salad dressing
2 tablespoons prepared mustard
1 pound (4 or 5 medium) cubed, cooked potatoes
3 hard-cooked eggs, coarsely chopped
¼ cup chopped ripe olives or pickles
2 tablespoons slivered green pepper
1 cup thinly sliced celery
1 small onion, diced
  Salt and pepper

Combine mayonnaise or salad dressing and mustard; add potatoes. Chill 2 to 3 hours to blend flavoring. Add eggs, olives or pickles, green pepper, celery, and onion. Season to taste. Chill. Yield: 6 servings.

Egg Salad–Stuffed Tomatoes

6 hard-cooked eggs
1 cup sliced celery
2 tablespoons minced green pepper
1 teaspoon minced onion
¼ cup mayonnaise
  Pinch chili powder
1 tablespoon vinegar
1 teaspoon salt
⅛ teaspoon pepper
6 tomatoes
  Parsley
  Lettuce

Cut eggs into medium-sized pieces. Then add rest of ingredients except tomatoes, parsley, and lettuce, and refrigerate. Before serving, wash chilled tomatoes, and remove cores. Then fill tomato cavities with egg salad, garnish with sprigs of parsley, and serve on lettuce. Yield: 6 servings.

Wilted Lettuce

3 slices bacon
½ cup vinegar
½ cup water
2 tablespoons sugar
1½ teaspoons salt
1 small onion, minced
1 egg, well beaten
Fresh leaf or head lettuce

Snip bacon into small pieces; sauté until crisp in large skillet. Stir in vinegar, water, sugar, salt, onion, and egg. Heat to boiling, stirring constantly. Wash and drain lettuce. Tear into small pieces. Toss with hot dressing in skillet. Yield: 6 servings.

Three-Bean Salad

⅔ cup vinegar
1 cup sugar
⅓ cup salad oil
1 fresh onion, chopped
1 (16-ounce) can green beans
1 (16-ounce) can yellow wax beans
or bean sprouts
1 (16-ounce) can kidney beans

Combine all ingredients. Let sit overnight in refrigerator. Drain well before serving. Yield: 8 to 10 servings.

Tomato Aspic

1½ tablespoons unflavored gelatin
¼ cup cold water
2½ cups tomato juice
1 tablespoon grated onion
3 whole cloves
1 bay leaf
¼ cup chopped celery
1 teaspoon chopped parsley
½ teaspoon salt
1 teaspoon sugar
2 teaspoons freshly squeezed lemon juice

Soften gelatin in the cold water. Mix the tomato juice with the seasonings, cover, and simmer 15 minutes. Strain, add the softened gelatin, and stir until dissolved. Pour into six individual molds. Chill until firm. Yield: 6 servings.

Celery Seed Dressing

1 teaspoon salt
1 teaspoon dry mustard
1 teaspoon paprika
1 teaspoon celery seed
½ cup light corn syrup
¼ to ⅓ cup vinegar
1 cup salad oil
1 tablespoon grated onion

Place all ingredients in a small bowl. Beat until well blended and thickened. Place in a covered container and chill for several hours. Yield: 1¾ cups.

Buttermilk Dressing

¼ cup buttermilk
¼ cup mayonnaise or salad dressing
1 teaspoon salt
⅛ teaspoon Worcestershire sauce
Dash paprika

Combine all ingredients and mix well. Serve over shredded cabbage. Yield: 6 servings.

Poppy Seed Dressing

1½ cups sugar
2 teaspoons dry mustard
2 teaspoons salt
⅔ cup vinegar
3 tablespoons onion juice
2 cups salad oil
3 tablespoons poppy seed

Mix sugar, mustard, salt, and vinegar. Add onion juice and stir in thoroughly. Use medium speed on mixer. Add oil slowly, beating constantly, and continue to beat until thick. Add poppy seed and beat for a few minutes. Store in a cool place or in the refrigerator, but not near freezing section. Yield: 2½ cups.

Dressing for Fruit Salad

  2 (3-ounce) packages cream cheese, softened
  1 cup mayonnaise
  1 cup cream, whipped
1½ cups chopped nuts

Cream together cream cheese and mayonnaise. Fold in whipped cream and chopped nuts. Use over fruit salads. Yield: 3½ cups.

Tomato Soup-
French Dressing

  1 (10½-ounce) can condensed tomato soup
  1 cup salad oil
  1 tablespoon black pepper
  1 tablespoon Worcestershire sauce
  1 tablespoon prepared mustard
  1 tablespoon garlic salt or 1 button garlic, cut fine
  1 teaspoon salt
 ½ cup sugar
 ½ cup vinegar

Pour soup into mixing bowl. Stir with spoon while adding other ingredients in order given. Place in covered jar in the refrigerator. Shake well each time before using. Yield: 3 cups.

Fruit Dressing

 ½ cup sugar
  1 tablespoon all-purpose flour
  1 egg yolk
     Juice of 1 lemon
 ½ cup unsweetened pineapple juice
  1 cup heavy cream, whipped

Combine sugar, flour, and egg yolk in top of double boiler. Add lemon and pineapple juices; cook until thick. Fold in whipped cream, and serve over fruit salad. Will keep for 3 days in refrigerator. Yield: 1½ cups.

Honey-Fruit Dressing

 ⅔ cup sugar
  1 teaspoon dry mustard
  1 teaspoon paprika
 ¼ teaspoon salt
  1 teaspoon ground celery seed
  1 tablespoon poppy seed
 ⅓ cup strained honey
  5 tablespoons cider vinegar
  1 tablespoon freshly squeezed lemon juice
  1 teaspoon grated onion
  1 cup salad oil

Mix dry ingredients; add honey, vinegar, lemon juice, and onion. Slowly pour oil into mixture, beating constantly until slightly creamy. Yield: 2 cups.

Low-Calorie French Dressing

  3 tablespoons salad oil
 ¾ teaspoon salt
  1 teaspoon sugar
 ⅛ teaspoon paprika
 ½ teaspoon dry mustard
 ¼ teaspoon Tabasco sauce
  1 cup grapefruit juice, divided
  2 teaspoons cornstarch

Combine salad oil, salt, sugar, paprika, mustard, and Tabasco sauce in mixing bowl. Blend ½ cup grapefruit juice and cornstarch in small saucepan. Cook over low heat, stirring constantly until mixture thickens and comes to a boil. Add to salad oil mixture; beat with rotary beater until smooth. Beat in remaining ½ cup grapefruit juice. Yield: 1½ cups.

Crab Imperial

1 tablespoon butter or margarine
1 cup cream
½ teaspoon salt
  Dash red pepper
½ teaspoon dry mustard
1 tablespoon Worcestershire sauce
1 teaspoon vinegar
1 cup finely chopped red and
  green pepper
¾ cup breadcrumbs
1 pound crabmeat

Melt butter or margarine; add cream, salt, red pepper, mustard, Worcestershire sauce, and vinegar. When thoroughly mixed and heated, add red and green peppers and breadcrumbs. Mix well. Remove from heat, and very gently mix in crabmeat. Stuff shells or baking dishes, mounding high, remembering not to break the lumps of crabmeat. Sprinkle lightly with breadcrumbs, and bake at 425° until brown. Yield: 6 to 8 servings.

Crab Newburg

2 (6½-ounce) cans crabmeat
¼ cup butter or margarine
½ cup cooking sherry
4 egg yolks
1¾ cups heavy cream
½ teaspoon salt
  Paprika
  Hot cooked rice

Remove any cartilage from crabmeat, being careful not to break meat chunks too small. Place crabmeat, butter, and cooking sherry in chafing dish or top of double boiler. Cook over direct heat, stirring gently, until liquid is reduced about half. Place slightly beaten egg yolks in cup and add cream to make 2 cups. Blend thoroughly. Add salt. Stir cream mixture into crab mixture. Place over hot water. Cook, stirring gently, until mixture thickens. If too thick, add more cream or a little milk. Sprinkle with paprika. Serve over hot rice. Yield: 6 servings.

Stuffed Crabs

18 medium crabs
4 tablespoons shortening
½ cup chopped green onions
2 cups breadcrumbs, divided
½ cup chopped celery
¼ cup minced parsley
1 teaspoon salt
½ teaspoon black pepper
¼ teaspoon red pepper
  Butter or margarine

Scald crabs and remove shells. Clean and place about six of the shells in boiling water, to which a bit of soda has been added. Let remain for about 10 minutes. Then remove and scrub shells, clean thoroughly, wash in clear water, and set aside to drain. Remove meat from crabs. Put shortening into deep frying pan and heat. Add onion, and cook slightly. Add 1½ cups breadcrumbs, chopped celery, parsley, crabmeat, and seasoning, mixing as added. Cook slowly over low heat for about 5 minutes; then put mixture into clean shells to bake. Put breadcrumbs on top of each, and dot with butter or margarine. Bake at 375° until top is browned. Yield: 6 servings.

Deviled Crabs

1 dozen fine, large crabs
½ pint cream
2 tablespoons all-purpose flour
1 tablespoon butter
  Yolks of 4 hard-cooked eggs, mashed fine
1 tablespoon salt
1 tablespoon chopped parsley
¼ teaspoon ground nutmeg
¼ teaspoon cayenne pepper
1 egg, beaten
  Breadcrumbs

Boil the crabs. Take out and drain after they have cooled in their own water. Break off the claws, separate the shells, remove the spongy portions of the fingers, and then pick out the meat. Put the cream on to boil, rub the flour and butter together well and add to the boiling cream. Stir and cook for 2 minutes.

Take from the heat and add the crabmeat and yolks of the hard-cooked eggs, mashed very fine. Add chopped parsley, ground nutmeg, salt, and cayenne. Clean the upper shells of the crabs, fill them with the mixture, brush over with a beaten egg, sprinkle with breadcrumbs, and brown in oven at 425°; or, better still, if you have a frying basket, plunge the crabs into the hot shortening until a nice brown. Yield: 6 servings.

Boiled Lobsters

1½ *gallons water*
 ⅓ *cup salt*
 6 *(1-pound) live lobsters*
    Melted butter or margarine

Place water in large container. Add salt. Cover and bring to the boiling point over high heat. Plunge lobsters headfirst into the boiling salted water. Cover and cook for 20 minutes. Drain. Crack claws. Serve with melted butter or margarine. Yield: 6 servings.

Broiled Boiled Lobsters

 2 *boiled lobsters*
 1 *tablespoon butter or margarine, melted*
    Dash white pepper
    Dash paprika
 ¼ *cup butter or margarine, melted*
 1 *tablespoon freshly squeezed lemon juice*

Lay lobsters open as flat as possible on a broiler pan. Brush lobster meat with the 1 tablespoon melted butter or margarine. Sprinkle with pepper and paprika.

Broil about 4 inches from source of heat for 5 minutes, or until lightly browned. Combine the ¼ cup melted butter or margarine and the lemon juice; serve with lobsters. Yield: 2 servings.

Fried Shad Fillets

 2 *pounds shad fillets*
 1 *egg, beaten*
 1 *tablespoon milk*
 1 *teaspoon salt*
 ½ *cup all-purpose flour*
 ½ *cup dry breadcrumbs*
    Shortening

Cut fish into serving-size portions. Combine egg, milk, and salt. Combine flour and crumbs. Dip fish in egg mixture and roll in flour and crumb mixture. Place fish in a heavy frying pan which contains about ⅛ inch of shortening, hot but not smoking. Fry. When fish is brown on one side, turn carefully and brown the other side. Cooking time: approximately 10 minutes, depending on thickness of fish. Drain on absorbent paper. Yield: 6 servings.

Baked Corn and Oysters

 1 *(17-ounce) can cream-style corn*
 1 *cup crackers, crushed*
 1 *beaten egg*
 ½ *teaspoon salt*
 ½ *cup milk or cream*
 ¼ *teaspoon black pepper*
 1 *teaspoon sugar*
 ¼ *cup melted butter*
 1 *cup small, fresh oysters*

Combine ingredients in order named. Pour the mixture into a greased 1½-quart baking dish and bake at 375° for 25 minutes. Do not overbake or oysters will become tough. Yield: 4 to 6 servings.

Fried Oysters

1 quart oysters
2 eggs, slightly beaten
2 tablespoons milk
1 teaspoon salt
⅛ teaspoon pepper
*1 cup breadcrumbs, cracker crumbs,
  or cornmeal*
Hot shortening for frying

Drain oysters. Mix egg and milk. Dip oysters in egg mixture, then in crumb or cornmeal mixture. Fry in deep, hot shortening; when brown on one side, turn and brown on other side. Serve hot. Yield: 6 servings.

Oyster Pie

¼ teaspoon celery salt
1 teaspoon onion juice
1 dozen oysters
2 cups white sauce
Pastry for 7-inch pie

Put celery, salt, onion juice and oysters in white sauce in 1-quart baking dish. Season to taste, cover with a rich piecrust, and bake at 450° for 20 minutes or until piecrust is done. Yield: 4 servings.

Oyster Jambalaya

3 teaspoons shortening
1 teaspoon all-purpose flour
1½ cups finely chopped onion
1 clove garlic, minced
1 cup chopped green pepper
¼ cup finely chopped celery
½ cup ground pork
½ pound ground veal
3 dozen oysters
2 teaspoons salt
¼ teaspoon black pepper
¼ teaspoon red pepper
2 cups cooked rice
1½ tablespoons finely chopped parsley
1½ tablespoons chopped onion tops

Make a golden brown roux with shortening and flour. Add onion, garlic, green pepper, and celery, and cook slowly until clear, stirring frequently. Add pork and veal and cook until brown, about 10 minutes. Drain liquid from oysters. Stir into vegetable mixture, and cook for 5 minutes. Add oysters, salt, black and red pepper. After 15 minutes, stir in rice. Transfer to top of double boiler to keep hot for 1 hour to let flavors blend. Before serving, stir in parsley and onion tops. Yield: 8 servings.

French Fried Shrimp

1½ pounds shrimp, fresh or frozen
2 eggs, beaten
1 teaspoon salt
½ cup all-purpose flour
½ cup dry breadcrumbs

Peel shrimp, leaving the last section of the shell on if desired. Cut almost through lengthwise and remove sand veins. Wash. Combine egg and salt. Dip each shrimp in egg, and roll in flour and crumb mixture. Fry in a basket in deep fat at 350° for 2 to 3 minutes or until golden brown. Drain on absorbent paper. Serve plain or with a sauce. Yield: 6 servings.

Cooked Shrimp
For Cocktails or Salad

8 cups water
¼ cup sliced onion
1 clove garlic
1 bay leaf
2 stalks celery with leaves
1½ tablespoons salt
⅛ teaspoon cayenne pepper
2 pounds shrimp
½ lemon, sliced

Simmer water, onion, garlic, bay leaf, celery, salt, and cayenne pepper for 15 minutes. Add shrimp and lemon. When water comes to a boil, cook for 5 minutes. Drain. Remove shells and make an incision down the back, then wash and remove black veins. Shrimp may then be used for cocktails, salads, or in dishes calling for cooked shrimp. Yield: 6 to 8 servings.

Shrimp Creole

¼ cup butter
1 cup coarsely chopped onions
1 cup diced celery
1 small clove garlic, finely minced
2 tablespoons all-purpose flour
1 teaspoon salt
1 teaspoon sugar
  Dash cayenne pepper
1 teaspoon paprika
½ small bay leaf
4 drops Tabasco sauce
½ cup diced green pepper
1 (1-pound, 3-ounce) can tomatoes
2 cups cooked, cleaned shrimp (1 pound fresh shrimp or 2 (7-ounce) cans
  Cheese Rice

Melt butter in fry pan. Add onion, celery, and garlic; cook slowly until tender but not brown. Add flour and seasonings; stir until blended. Stir in green pepper and tomatoes. Cook for 10 minutes over low heat, stirring occasionally. Add shrimp and heat. Serve in hot casserole lined with Cheese Rice. Yield: 6 servings.

Cheese Rice

3 cups water
1 tablespoon butter
1 teaspoon salt
1½ cups uncooked regular rice
2 cups shredded American cheese
2 tablespoons finely chopped onion
1 teaspoon prepared mustard

Bring water to boiling point. Add butter, salt, and rice; bring to a boil, reduce heat to low and cook covered for 20 to 25 minutes or until tender. Stir cheese, onion, and mustard into hot rice.

Shrimp Bisque

¾ pound cooked shrimp
2 tablespoons chopped onion
2 tablespoons chopped celery
¼ cup butter or margarine
2 tablespoons all-purpose flour
1 teaspoon salt
¼ teaspoon paprika
⅛ teaspoon black pepper
4 cups milk
  Parsley

Grind shrimp. Cook onion and celery in butter or margarine until tender. Blend in flour and seasonings. Add milk gradually and cook until thick, stirring constantly. Add shrimp; heat. Garnish with chopped parsley sprinkled over the top. Yield: 6 servings.

Red Snapper With Shrimp Stuffing

Select a fish weighing 3 to 4 pounds. Have fish dressed. Clean, rub salt inside and out, and stuff with Shrimp Stuffing. Fasten together with skewers, or lace with string to hold in place.

Brush fish with melted fat and place in greased baking pan. Bake at 350° for about 40 minutes, or until fish flakes easily when tested with a fork.

Shrimp Stuffing

¼ cup chopped celery
2 tablespoons chopped onion
2 tablespoons butter or margarine
3 slices cooked bacon, minced
1 cup soft breadcrumbs
½ cup chopped shrimp
1 egg
  Salt and pepper

Sauté celery and onion in butter or margarine until soft. Add remaining ingredients and mix well. Yield: stuffing for 3- to 4-pound fish.

Shrimp Addie

6 strips bacon
2 to 2¼ cups cooked tomatoes
2 large green peppers, cut into strips
1 clove garlic, finely chopped (optional)
2 cups boiled peeled shrimp (1 pound in shell)
Hot cooked rice or grits

Cook bacon in heavy skillet until brown and crisp; remove from skillet and drain. Add tomatoes, green peppers, and garlic to skillet; simmer until peppers are tender and tomatoes are reduced to about one-half (about 40 minutes). Add shrimp, and simmer 5 minutes longer or until thoroughly hot. Serve with either hot rice or grits. Yield: 4 servings.

South Louisiana Shrimp

2 pounds shrimp
1 small onion
1 clove garlic
½ tablespoon vinegar
Water to cover shrimp
Sauce

Boil shrimp and other ingredients, but do not overcook. To do this, drop shrimp into boiling water and allow to return to boiling point; and cook for exactly 8 minutes. Drain, peel, and devein in ice water. Marinate the shrimp in Sauce for 2 hours before serving. Yield: 8 servings.

Sauce

1 clove garlic, mashed
Juice of 1 freshly squeezed lemon
1 cup olive oil
½ teaspoon salt
Dash Tabasco sauce
2 or 3 drops Worcestershire sauce
1 tablespoon mustard
Catsup to suit taste

Combine ingredients and blend. Yield: sauce for 8 servings of shrimp.

Shrimp and Rice

1 pound shrimp
1 teaspoon Worcestershire sauce
2 tablespoons all-purpose flour
1 teaspoon paprika
¼ cup butter or margarine
½ cup chopped celery
⅓ cup chopped green pepper
¼ cup minced onion
3 cups hot cooked rice
4 slices bacon
Salt and pepper to taste

Clean and devein shrimp; sprinkle with Worcestershire sauce. Roll in mixture of flour and paprika. Melt butter in large skillet. Add celery, green pepper, and onion, and cook over low heat for about 5 minutes. Add shrimp; increase heat and cook for about 5 minutes more, or until flour browns and shrimp turn pink. Add hot rice and a small amount of water, if needed. Fry bacon until crisp, crumble and add with bacon drippings to shrimp. Add salt and pepper to taste. Serve hot. Yield: 4 servings.

Broiled Fish

2 pounds fillets or steaks
   (bass, trout, snapper, etc.)
1 teaspoon salt
⅛ teaspoon pepper
4 tablespoons melted butter

Cut fish into serving-size portions. Sprinkle both sides with salt and pepper. Place fish on preheated greased broiler pan about 2 inches from heat, skin-side up, unless skin has been removed. Brush with melted butter. Broil for 5 to 8 minutes or until slightly brown; baste with melted butter. Turn carefully and brush with melted butter. Cook for 5 to 8 minutes, or until fish flakes easily when tested with a fork. Remove carefully to a hot platter and serve immediately. Yield: 4 to 6 servings.

Baked Stuffed Fish

1 (3- to 4-pound) fish, dressed
1½ teaspoons salt
3 tablespoons chopped onion
¾ cup celery, chopped
6 tablespoons melted butter or margarine
⅛ teaspoon pepper
1 teaspoon thyme, sage, or savory seasoning
4 cups breadcrumbs

Clean, wash, and dry fish. Sprinkle inside and out with salt. Cook the onions and celery in melted butter or margarine for about 10 minutes, or until tender. Add cooked vegetables and seasonings to breadcrumbs, and mix thoroughly. Add water, if needed to moisten. Stuff fish loosely with dressing, and sew the opening with needle or string, or close with skewers. Place fish in a greased baking pan. Brush with melted fat and bake at 350° for 40 to 60 minutes, or until fish flakes easily when tested with a fork. Baste with melted butter or margarine occasionally during baking, if fish seems dry. Remove string or skewers and serve hot. Yield: 6 servings.

Pan Fried Fish

2 pounds fillets, or 6 small pan-dressed fish
1 teaspoon salt
⅛ teaspoon pepper
1 tablespoon milk or water
1 egg, slightly beaten
1 cup cornmeal
   Salad oil or melted shortening

Sprinkle both sides of fish with salt and pepper. Combine milk and beaten egg. Dip fish in this mixture, then in cornmeal. Heat ⅛-inch oil or shortening in heavy skillet or frying pan. When hot, but not smoking, fry fish at moderate heat. When brown on one side, turn carefully and brown on other side. Total cooking time will be about 10 minutes, depending on thickness of fish. Remove from pan, and drain on absorbent paper. Serve immediately. Yield: 4 to 6 servings.

Salmon Loaf

2 cups (1-pound can) drained flaked salmon
1½ cups fine dry breadcrumbs
1 (10½-ounce) can condensed cream of celery soup
½ cup minced green pepper
2 eggs, slightly beaten

Combine all ingredients; pack lightly into a greased loafpan (9 x 5 x 3 inches). Bake at 350° for about 1 hour. Yield: 6 servings.

Dove Pie

6 doves
4 cups water
1 onion, chopped
1 small bunch parsley, chopped
3 whole cloves
2 tablespoons all-purpose flour
2 tablespoons butter or margarine
  Salt and pepper
  Pastry for double crust pie

Place doves in a saucepan; cover with water; add onion, parsley, and cloves. Cook until tender. Remove doves. Skim liquid and thicken it with a paste made of flour and butter or margarine. Season to taste with salt and pepper. Line a baking dish with pastry and place birds in dish. Cover with gravy. Top with pastry. Bake at 350° for 1 hour. Yield: 4 to 6 servings.

Dove Hash à la Reith

4 cups diced, cooked breasts of doves
1 (10½-ounce) can chicken consomme
6 tablespoons butter, divided
2½ tablespoons all-purpose flour
⅔ cup cream
⅔ cup breadcrumbs
⅔ cup chopped green pepper
⅔ cup chopped onion
2 tablespoons chopped parsley
½ teaspoon ground sage
½ teaspoon salt
  Freshly ground black pepper to taste
2 ounces sherry wine

Cook whole doves in chicken consomme until tender. Remove breasts and dice meat. Measure 4 cups and set aside. Blend 3 tablespoons butter with flour and cream. Sauté breadcrumbs, green pepper, onion, parsley, and sage in remaining 3 tablespoons butter. Mix the sautéed ingredients, flour mixture, and dove meat. Place in skillet. Add salt, pepper, and sherry, and let cook gently for 25 or 30 minutes. Before serving, put into a casserole dish and cook for a few minutes under the broiler. To keep right consistency while sautéing, add pot liquor left from cooking whole doves. Yield: 4 to 6 servings.

Roast Doves

14 to 16 doves
  Salt and pepper to taste
  All-purpose flour
½ cup salad oil
½ cup chopped green onions
1½ cups water
1 cup sherry
¼ cup chopped parsley

Dredge doves in seasoned flour. Brown in oil in heavy roaster in a 400° oven. Add chopped onions and water. Cover. Reduce heat to 350°; cook until tender. Add sherry and baste often during cooking. Add chopped parsley to gravy before serving. Yield: 6 to 8 servings.

Doves Brazos Valley

6 doves
1½ sticks melted butter
1 tablespoon Worcestershire sauce
1 teaspoon garlic salt
⅓ cup cooking sherry
1 cup chopped mushrooms
½ teaspoon ground nutmeg
  Salt and pepper to taste
⅓ cup all-purpose flour
  Toast

Brown doves on all sides in melted butter in a large skillet. After doves become brown, add remaining ingredients, except flour, to drippings to make sauce. Cover skillet. Allow to simmer for about 20 minutes. Remove the doves from skillet; add flour to the sauce to make a roux. Place doves on toast and top with sauce. Yield: 3 servings.

Roast Wild Duck

2 wild ducks
1 onion, quartered
1 apple, quartered
3 stalks celery, cut into long strips
1 cup finely chopped celery
1 cup finely chopped onion
1 cup seeded raisins
1 cup coarsely chopped pecans
4 cups soft breadcrumbs
½ teaspoon salt
2 eggs, beaten
½ cup scalded milk
6 slices bacon

The day before ducks are to be roasted, stuff cavity with quartered onion and apple and celery stalks, cut into large pieces. Let stand in refrigerator overnight. Next morning combine chopped celery, onion, raisins, and pecans with breadcrumbs and salt. Add eggs and mix well. Add scalded milk and blend.
Remove stuffing and weigh ducks. Stuff with breadcrumb dressing. Sew up all openings. Place 3 strips of bacon across breast of each duck in an uncovered roasting pan. Roast at 500° for 15 minutes, then reduce heat to 300° and roast, allowing 30 minutes per pound. Yield: 4 to 6 servings.

Braised Venison

Dredge well with flour and sear on all sides in shortening. Add enough water to cover the bottom of pan; add 1 tablespoon vinegar. Cover tightly and cook very slowly for about 2 hours, adding a little more liquid as necessary. About 30 minutes before meat is tender, add ½ cup each of chopped celery, apple, carrot, and onion. This mixture will flavor the gravy and add flavor to meat, absorbing some of the gamy flavor. It may be strained from the gravy before serving, if desired.

Venison Pot Roast

3 to 4 pounds venison (shoulder, rump, round)
  All-purpose flour
  Salt and pepper
  Shortening
5 whole carrots
5 whole potatoes
5 whole onions
  Turnips or celery, if desired

Dredge meat with flour, add salt and pepper, and brown in hot shortening. Braise the meat for 2 to 3 hours over low heat (small amount of water in covered skillet). When meat is tender, add the vegetables, and more hot water if necessary, and cook until vegetables are done. Make a gravy of the liquid in the pan and pour over the meat and vegetables. Yield: 6 to 8 servings.

Venison Chili

½ pound suet
2 large onions, chopped
1 large garlic clove, minced
5 tablespoons all-purpose flour
¼ cup chili powder
1 teaspoon cumin
  Cubes of venison for 8 to 10 servings
½ teaspoon oregano
1 bay leaf
3 (8-ounce) cans tomato paste
2 cups canned tomatoes
1 tablespoon salt
1 teaspoon pepper
6 chili peppers, chopped

Cook suet in skillet, then remove cracklings. Add onions and garlic and cook until soft, but not brown.

Mix flour, chili powder, and cumin in a paper bag. Add cubes of venison and shake until each piece is coated. Add to onion and cook until brown. Add other ingredients and simmer for 4 to 5 hours, stirring occasionally and adding hot water as needed. Yield: 8 to 10 servings.

Roast Duck

2 ducks, cut in half
  Garlic
  Salt and pepper
1 cup chopped celery
1 large onion, chopped
1 or 2 cloves garlic, chopped
1 cup chili sauce
1 tablespoon Worcestershire sauce
1 tablespoon dry mustard
½ tablespoon ground nutmeg
  Juice of 1 small lemon
2 cups water
  Paprika

Rub ducks with garlic, salt, and pepper. Place breast-side down in roaster. Combine other ingredients except paprika; pour over ducks. Bake at 325° for 3 hours. When ducks are tender, turn breast-side up and sprinkle with paprika. Bake until golden brown. Serve gravy with ducks. If a thickened gravy is desired, add a small amount of flour to drippings and cook until thickened. Yield: 4 servings.

Creole Game Stew

3 ducks (teal, butterball, or mallards are best)
4 tablespoons all-purpose flour
  Salt and pepper to taste
4 tablespoons peanut oil
½ cup chopped onion
¾ cup chopped green pepper
¼ cup all-purpose flour
3 chicken bouillon cubes
3 cups hot water

Cut ducks into serving-size pieces. Dredge with 4 tablespoons flour, salt, and pepper. Brown in peanut oil in a heavy skillet. Remove ducks. Add onion and green pepper and cook until flour is browned. Add bouillon cubes to hot water and stir until dissolved. Add to browned flour mixture in skillet, along with ducks and vegetables. Cook over low heat for 1½ to 2 hours.

Serve with hot fluffy rice tossed with chopped parsley or chopped green pepper. Yield: 3 to 6 servings.

Barbecued Duck

1 cup salad oil
½ cup vinegar
¼ cup soy sauce
6 cloves garlic, crushed
1 sprig rosemary
1 tablespoon celery seed
  Salt and pepper to taste
4 wild ducks

Combine first seven ingredients to make sauce, and simmer for about 10 minutes. Cut ducks into halves and barbecue, turning several times and basting generously with sauce until tender. Yield: 8 to 10 servings.

Braised Quail with Bacon

6 quail
18 strips bacon
2 tablespoons butter or margarine
½ cup hot water
4 tablespoons all-purpose flour
6 slices toast

Prepare quail for cooking, cover, and let stand overnight in refrigerator. The next day, cover quail with salted water, using 1 tablespoon salt for each quart water. Let stand for 15 minutes; drain and dry inside and out with a cloth. Place 1 strip bacon in cavity of each bird and place in shallow roasting pan. Place a strip of bacon over breast of each and a strip over the legs. Bake at 450° for 5 minutes; reduce heat to 350° and continue cooking for 40 minutes, basting frequently with a mixture of the butter and hot water. At the end of the baking time, sprinkle with flour, increase heat to 450°, and brown for about 10 minutes. Serve on toast. Yield: 6 servings.

Ranch-Style Creamed Quail

12 quail
   Salt and pepper
 1 pound butter or margarine
 4 cups sweet cream
 1 to 1½ cups toasted breadcrumbs

Salt and pepper cleaned, dressed quail; simmer slowly in butter in cooker until tender. Add cream and continue simmering until done. Remove quail to hot platter. Sift toasted breadcrumbs over quail. Pour cream gravy from cooker over quail. Yield: 12 servings.

Smothered Quail

 6 quail
 6 tablespoons butter or margarine
 3 tablespoons all-purpose flour
 2 cups chicken broth
½ cup sherry wine
   Salt and pepper to taste
   Cooked rice

Prepare quail; brown in heavy skillet or Dutch oven in 6 tablespoons butter or margarine. Remove quail to baking dish. Add flour to butter in skillet and stir well. Slowly add chicken broth, sherry, and salt and pepper to taste; blend well and pour over quail. Cover baking dish and bake at 350° for about 1 hour. Serve with cooked rice. Yield: 6 servings.

Baked Quail

 6 quail
   Water
 4 tablespoons Worcestershire sauce
 1 teaspoon Tabasco sauce
 3 tablespoons olive oil
   Juice of 3 lemons
½ stick butter
 2 tablespoons molasses
   Salt and pepper to taste
 1 teaspoon prepared mustard

Place quail in roasting pan with enough water to cover bottom of the pan. Cover and place in 300° oven. Combine other ingredients and blend together over low heat. When quail have cooked for 30 minutes, remove from oven and pour sauce over birds. Return to oven, cover, and continue cooking 30 to 40 minutes longer, basting frequently. During the last 10 minutes of cooking time, remove cover to brown birds and thicken the sauce. Yield: 6 servings.

Hunters' Sautéed Quail

 6 club rolls
¾ cup butter, divided
 6 quail, split
 1 teaspoon salt
   Freshly ground black pepper
   Fruit Sauce

Split rolls in half and hollow out centers. Toast in a 325° oven until brown. Melt ¼ cup butter and brush the rolls with the butter. Sauté the quail over high heat in the remaining ½ cup of butter for 10 minutes or until golden brown. Sprinkle with salt and pepper. Arrange quail on rolls and serve with Fruit Sauce. Yield: 6 servings.

Fruit Sauce

 1 cup seedless white grapes
 1 cup water
 4 tablespoons butter or margarine
½ cup port wine
⅛ teaspoon ground cloves
½ teaspoon ground ginger
 2 tablespoons finely chopped mushrooms
½ cup finely chopped filberts

Put grapes into 1 cup water and bring to a boil. Cover, reduce heat, and simmer for 5 minutes. Drain off water. Add butter, wine, cloves, and ginger to grapes. Cover and simmer for 5 minutes. Stir in mushrooms and simmer for 5 minutes. Add filberts (hazelnuts), and serve immediately. Yield: 6 servings.

Roast Quail

    4 quail
    4 slices bacon
    1 tablespoon butter or margarine
    ½ cup hot water
      Juice of half lemon
    1 (3-ounce) can broiled
      mushrooms, drained

Wipe excess moisture off the quail, inside and out. Bind each bird with a slice of bacon. Place birds in a buttered pan and roast at 350° for about 30 minutes, or until tender. Baste occasionally. Remove birds; add butter or margarine, water, and lemon juice to drippings, stirring to make a gravy. Add mushrooms. Serve birds on toast with gravy poured over them. Yield: 2 to 4 servings.

Venison, Hunter's Style

    3 pounds venison
      Salt and pepper
    2 tablespoons butter or margarine
    1 onion, chopped
    1 (1-inch) cube ham, minced
    1 clove garlic, minced
    2 bay leaves
    2 sprigs thyme, crushed
    1 tablespoon all-purpose flour
    2 cups warm water
    4 cups consomme
    ½ pound fresh mushrooms, chopped
      Grated rind of 1 lemon

Cut venison into pieces 2 inches square. Salt and pepper generously. Heat butter in skillet and brown vension slowly. When almost brown, add onion; brown slightly. Then add ham, garlic, bay leaves, and thyme. Stir and simmer for 2 minutes. Add the flour and cook a few minutes longer.

Add warm water and let cool to a good simmer. Add consomme and cook slowly for 1 hour. Season again according to taste; then add mushrooms and grated lemon rind. Let cook for 30 minutes longer. Serve on a very hot plate. Yield: 8 servings.

Venison Meatballs

    1 pound ground venison
    ½ pound ground pork
    ½ cup fine, dry breadcrumbs
    1 egg, beaten
    ½ cup cooked mashed potatoes
    1 teaspoon seasoned salt
    ½ teaspoon brown sugar
    ¼ teaspoon pepper
    ¼ teaspoon ground allspice
    ¼ teaspoon ground nutmeg
    ⅛ teaspoon ground cloves
    ⅛ teaspoon ground ginger
    3 tablespoons butter or margarine

Combine all ingredients except butter. Mix well and shape into balls about 1 inch in diameter. Melt butter in skillet over low heat. Add meatballs and brown on all sides, shaking pan now and then. Cover with tightly fitting lid and cook over low heat for 15 minutes. Yield: 6 to 8 servings.

Squirrel Stew

    3 squirrels
    2 onions, chopped
    1 green pepper, chopped
    2 medium potatoes, diced
    ¼ cup diced celery
    4 tablespoons chili powder
      Salt and pepper to taste
      Dash Louisiana hot sauce
    1 cup cooked rice

Cover squirrels with water and cook until tender. Remove from water and cool; reserve broth. Remove meat from bones and put back into broth. Bring to a boil and add all other ingredients except rice. Cook for about 45 minutes or until vegetables are tender. Add cooked rice. Serve hot. Yield: 6 servings.

Country-Style Squirrel

2 squirrels
  Salt and pepper to taste
  All-purpose flour
3 tablespoons shortening
2 cups water

Cut squirrels into serving-size pieces and shake in a paper bag containing salt, pepper, and flour to dredge well. Fry in skillet until golden brown. Remove squirrel from skillet and pour off all drippings except 2 teaspoonfuls. Add water and bring to a boil. Return squirrel to skillet; cover, and cook over low heat for about 1 hour, until meat almost leaves bone. Turn squirrel occasionally and baste often. Yield: 3 to 4 servings.

Venison Burgers

2½ pounds ground venison
  ½ cup minced onion
  1 clove garlic, minced
  4 tablespoons chopped parsley
⅔ cup dry red wine
  2 tablespoons soy sauce
  Salt and pepper to taste
  Hamburger buns

Mix all ingredients; form into thick patties. Cook on barbecue grill, 4 inches from coals, or broil in oven, 10 minutes on each side (less for rare burgers). Serve immediately in hot hamburger buns. Yield: 8 to 10 servings.

Smoked Wild Turkey

Rub 10- to 15-pound wild turkey with curing salt. Refrigerate for 5 days in a plastic bag. Then wash turkey thoroughly inside and out being careful to remove all the salt. The turkey must be smoked in a covered barbecue pit using dampened hickory sawdust. Add sawdust to the fire from time to time to keep the smoke going. Smoke for 36 hours, turning every now and then. Baste every hour during the daytime with a mixture containing equal parts of cola beverage, vinegar, and white wine.

Wild Turkey

Dry pick and singe wild turkey. Wash with warm water (4 teaspoons soda to the gallon). Remove tendons. Soak the fowl in salt water (4 tablespoons salt to the gallon of water) for 3 to 3½ hours. Pour off salt water, wash turkey, and rub well with lemon juice. Make a paste of butter and flour — 8 to 10 tablespoons butter to 1 cup flour. Spread paste over the turkey. Place bird in 475° to 500° oven and brown quickly to set the paste. Stuff bird with dressing.

Dressing for Wild Turkey

4 cups breadcrumbs (half cornbread and half biscuit and light bread)
2 cups diced celery
1 cup chopped onion
2 tablespoons freshly squeezed lemon juice
1 teaspoon salt
¼ teaspoon red pepper
½ teaspoon Worcestershire sauce
½ teaspoon steak sauce
1 to 1½ cups butter
1 cup hot water

Combine breadcrumbs, celery, onion, lemon juice, salt and pepper. Blend Worcestershire sauce and steak sauce with butter and add to mixture. Stuff turkey and place in roaster with 1 cup hot water. Cover and bake at 325° for 30 minutes to the pound. When turkey is almost tender, remove cover and brown. Make gravy from drippings when bird is done. Yield: 6 to 8 servings.

Roasting Chart For Beef
Roasting at $300°$ to $325°$

Cut	Approximate Weight (Pounds)	Meat Thermometer Reading (Degrees)	Approximate Cooking Time* (Minutes Per Pound)
Standing Rib[1]	6 to 8	140 (rare) 160 (medium) 170 (well)	23 to 25 27 to 30 32 to 35
Standing Rib[1]	4 to 6	140 (rare) 160 (medium) 170 (well)	26 to 30 34 to 38 40 to 42
Rolled Rib	5 to 7	140 (rare) 160 (medium) 170 (well)	32 38 48
Rib Eye[2] (Delmonico)	4 to 6	140 (rare) 160 (medium) 170 (well)	18 to 20 20 to 22 22 to 24
Tenderloin, whole[3]	4 to 6	140 (rare)	45 to 60 (total)
Tenderloin, half[3]	2 to 3	140 (rare)	45 to 50 (total)
Rolled rump (high quality)	4 to 6	150 to 170	25 to 30
Sirloin tip (high quality)	3½ to 4 6 to 8	140 to 170 140 to 170	35 to 40 30 to 35
Beef loaf (9 x 5 inches)	1½ to 2½	160 to 170	1 to 1½ hrs.

*Based on meat taken directly from the refrigerator.
[1]Ribs which measure 6 to 7 inches from chine bone to tip of rib.
[2]Roast at $350°$ oven temperature.
[3]Roast at $425°$ oven temperature.

Roasting Chart For Beef
Cooking in Liquid

Cut	Approximate Weight (Pounds)	Approximate Total Cooking Time (Hours)
Fresh or corned beef	4 to 6	3½ to 4½
Cross-cut shanks	¾ to 1¼	2½ to 3
Beef for stew		2½ to 3½

Pot Roast with Vegetables

- 1 (4- to 5-pound) beef chuck roast
  Salt and pepper
  All-purpose flour
- 3 tablespoons shortening
- ¼ teaspoon thyme or marjoram
- ½ cup chopped onions
- ½ cup water
- 8 medium carrots
- 8 small onions
- 4 medium potatoes, quartered

Sprinkle roast with salt and pepper and dredge in flour. Melt shortening in heavy skillet, and brown roast slowly and thoroughly. Sprinkle meat with thyme and chopped onions. Add water, cover tightly, and cook slowly over low heat for 2½ hours, or until meat is almost tender. Turn meat two or three times during cooking, and add small amounts of water when necessary. Add vegetables, and sprinkle with salt and pepper. Cover, and cook until meat and vegetables are tender — about 20 minutes. To make gravy, dilute drippings with water, and thicken with a flour and water paste. Yield: 6 to 8 servings.

Beef Stroganoff

- 2 pounds beef for stew, cut in pieces
  ½ inch wide
- 6 tablespoons all-purpose flour
- 1½ teaspoons salt
- ¼ teaspoon pepper
- 3 tablespoons shortening
- 1 cup chopped onions
- 1 cup tomato juice
- 2 cups liquid (water and liquid
  from mushrooms)
- 1 (4-ounce) can button mushrooms
- 3 tablespoons all-purpose flour
- 1 cup commercial sour cream
  Cooked noodles or rice

Dredge meat with flour seasoned with salt and pepper; brown in shortening. Add chopped onions and brown. Pour off drippings. Add tomato juice and 1½ cups liquid. Cover and cook slowly for 1½ hours. Add mushrooms. Thicken with flour added to the remaining ½ cup liquid, stirring constantly. Fold in sour cream. Serve over cooked noodles or rice. Yield: 6 to 8 servings.

Brisket of Beef

- 1 (4- to 5-pound) brisket of beef
- 2 medium onions, sliced
- 1 bay leaf
- 5 carrots
  Salt and pepper
  Boiling water
- 1 stalk celery
  Horseradish Sauce

Place meat in a heavy kettle, add seasonings and vegetables, and enough boiling water to cover. Bring to a boil, then reduce heat. Cook slowly until tender, about 3 to 4 hours. Slice meat and serve in Horseradish Sauce. Yield: 4 to 6 servings.

Horseradish Sauce

- 1 large onion, chopped
- 4 tablespoons butter or margarine
- 2 tablespoons all-purpose flour
- 2 cups soup stock
- 1 cup fresh horseradish
- 1 cup vinegar
- 2 cloves
- 2 bay leaves
- 1 teaspoon salt
  Pepper
- ½ cup sugar

Sauté onion in melted butter or margarine until brown. Add flour and soup stock gradually, then add remaining ingredients. Heat the meat in the sauce.

Italian Spaghetti

1   pound ground beef
2   medium onions, chopped
½   large green pepper, chopped
1   tablespoon butter
1   (20-ounce) can tomatoes
1   (6-ounce) can tomato paste
1   (4-ounce) can mushrooms
1   clove garlic, chopped
1   tablespoon Worcestershire sauce
1   tablespoon (or more) chili powder
    Salt and pepper to taste
1   (7-ounce) package spaghetti
    Parmesan cheese

Fry ground beef, chopped onions, and pepper in butter until slightly browned. Add canned tomatoes, tomato paste, mushrooms, chopped garlic, Worcestershire sauce, chili powder, and salt and pepper to taste. Simmer over low heat for 3 to 4 hours. If desired, cook, package, and freeze.

Cook spaghetti according to directions on box. Serve by pouring meat sauce over spaghetti, then sprinkling with Parmesan cheese. Yield: 6 to 8 servings.

Southern Baked Hash

1   large onion, sliced thin
1   green pepper, sliced thin
2   tablespoons butter or margarine
1   pound ground beef
¼   cup regular rice, uncooked
1   cup canned tomatoes
½   teaspoon salt
½   teaspoon chili powder
¼   teaspoon pepper

Fry onion and pepper in butter or margarine until brown. Remove from skillet. Put ground meat into skillet and cook until meat is browned; add onion and pepper. Stir rice, tomatoes, salt, chili powder, and pepper into the meat. Bake uncovered in a greased 2-quart casserole at 350° for 1 hour. Yield: 3 to 4 servings.

Creole Meat Loaf

1½ pounds ground beef
½   pound ground pork
1   small green pepper, grated
2   eggs, beaten
1   small onion, grated
1   cup milk
1   cup toasted breadcrumbs
    Salt and pepper
1   tablespoon Worcestershire sauce
    Creole Sauce

Mix ingredients thoroughly in the order given and shape into a loaf. Pack into a greased 9- x 5- x 4-inch loaf pan; cover with Creole Sauce, and bake at 350° for 1 hour. Yield: 6 to 8 servings.

Creole Sauce

2   tablespoons shortening
2   tablespoons all-purpose flour
½   green pepper, chopped
½   small onion, chopped
1   clove garlic, chopped
1   cup milk
2   cups canned tomatoes
    Salt and pepper
1   tablespoon Worcestershire sauce

Melt shortening; add flour, and cook over medium heat until a rich brown, stirring constantly. Add chopped pepper, onion, and garlic. Let simmer until wilted; add milk. Add tomatoes, salt, pepper, and Worcestershire sauce. Let come to a boil and cook for 4 to 5 minutes. Yield: 2½ cups.

Swiss Steak with Vegetables

2   pounds round or chuck steak
½   cup all-purpose flour
2   teaspoons salt
⅛   teaspoon pepper
1   small onion, chopped
3   tablespoons shortening
1   cup tomatoes
1½ cups sliced carrots
1½ cups chopped celery

Cut steak at least 1½ inches thick. Mix flour, salt, and pepper, and thoroughly pound into steak. Brown meat and onion in hot shortening. Add tomatoes. Cover and bake at 350° for about 1 hour and 45 minutes. Add carrots and celery 45 minutes before removing from oven. Yield: 6 servings.

Meat Loaf

1½ pounds ground beef
½ (10½-ounce) can condensed
      tomato soup
 1 cup cracker crumbs
 2 stalks celery, chopped
 1 egg
½ cup cubed American cheese
 1 large onion, chopped
½ medium green pepper, chopped
1½ teaspoons salt
¼ teaspoon pepper
      American cheese slices
¼ cup water
½ (10½-ounce) can condensed
      tomato soup

Combine first 10 ingredients. Mix well and form into one large or two small meat loaves. Freeze if desired, and bake without thawing. Just unwrap, place in greased baking dish, and top with slices of American cheese. Combine water and tomato soup and pour over cheese slices. Bake at 350° for 45 minutes. Yield: 8 to 10 servings.

Stuffed Flank Steak

 1 (1½- to 2-pound) flank steak
 1 teaspoon salt
 1 cup breadcrumbs
¼ cup chopped onion
 1 teaspoon poultry seasoning
½ cup chopped celery
¼ cup shortening, melted
 1 cup water

Select a flank steak weighing 1½ to 2 pounds. Sprinkle salt on steak. Make a stuffing by combining breadcrumbs, onion, poultry seasoning, celery, and

melted shortening. Spread over the steak. Roll steak crosswise and fasten edges with metal skewers to hold in the stuffing. Brown the steak on all sides in a small amount of shortening, in heavy skillet. Add 1 cup water and cover skillet. Bake at 350° for 2 hours. To serve, cut across the roll in 1-inch slices. Yield: 3 servings.

Braised Short Ribs of Beef

Place short ribs of beef in a roasting pan. Season with salt and pepper. Brown in a 400° oven for 20 minutes. Add ½ cup water and cover closely. Reduce temperature to 300° and cook slowly until tender, about 1½ hours.

Braised Stuffed Beef Heart

 1 beef heart
¼ cup shortening
¼ cup chopped celery
 2 tablespoons chopped onion
 2 tablespoons chopped parsley
 3 to 4 cups breadcrumbs
½ teaspoon salt
½ teaspoon savory
      Pepper to taste
 2 cups water

Wash the heart and remove fat. Make a slit in the center of the heart and remove veins, arteries, and gristle. Set aside to prepare the stuffing. Melt shortening and add celery, onion, and parsley. Cook for a few minutes and add breadcrumbs. Add salt, savory, and pepper. Fill the heart cavity with the stuffing, and fasten together with metal skewers and string, or by sewing. Brown the heart in a small amount of shortening. Place in a Dutch oven, add water, and cover. Bake at 300° for about 4 hours. Use liquid for gravy. Yield: 8 servings.

Roasting Chart For Fresh Pork
Roasting at 300° to 350°

Cut	Approximate Weight (Pounds)	Meat Thermometer Reading (Degrees)	Approximate Cooking Time (Minutes Per Pound)
Loin			
Center	3 to 5	170	30 to 35
Half	5 to 7	170	35 to 40
End	3 to 4	170	40 to 45
Roll	3 to 5	170	35 to 40
Boneless Top	2 to 4	170	30 to 35
Crown	4 to 6	170	35 to 40
Picnic Shoulder			
Bone-In	5 to 8	170	30 to 35
Rolled	3 to 5	170	35 to 40
Boston Shoulder	4 to 6	170	40 to 45
Leg (fresh ham)			
Whole (bone-in)	12 to 16	170	22 to 26
Whole (boneless)	10 to 14	170	24 to 28
Half (bone-in)	5 to 8	170	35 to 40
Tenderloin	½ to 1		45 to 60
Country-style backbones		Well Done	Hours 1½ to 2½
Spareribs			1½ to 2½

Pork Crown Roast

1 (6- to 10-pound) crown roast of pork
loin (14 to 16 ribs)
Salt
Pepper

Have your butcher fashion a pork crown roast at the market. He will tie the roast to form a circle with ends of rib bones exposed. Be sure the backbone is removed for easy carving. Season with salt and pepper. Place crown roast, rib ends down, on rack in open roasting pan. Do not add water and do not cover. Roast at 325° for 2 hours. Remove from oven.

Invert roast so that rib ends are up. Insert roast meat thermometer into cen-ter of the thickest part of roast, making certain that it does not rest in fat or on bone. Continue roasting until meat thermometer registers 170°. Remove roast to heated platter; garnish.

Allow roast to "rest" at room temperature for 15 minutes before carving. Slice between ribs. One rib section will make a serving for one person. Yield: 14 to 16 servings.

Dixie Pork Chops

8 pork chops
  About 3 tablespoons shortening
½ teaspoon salt
½ teaspoon sage
4 apples, cored and cut in rings
¼ cup brown sugar
2 tablespoons all-purpose flour
1 cup hot water
  Few drops vinegar
½ cup seedless raisins

Brown chops in hot shortening. Remove chops and save fat. Put chops in baking dish; sprinkle with salt and sage. Top with apple rings and sprinkle with sugar. In skillet blend fat, flour, water, and vinegar and cook until thick. Add raisins; pour over the chops. Bake in uncovered baking dish at 350° for 1 hour. Yield: 8 servings.

Georgia Hot Sausage Pie

1 pound hot pork sausage
2 cups canned tomatoes
2 cups whole-kernel corn, drained
2 tablespoons minced onion
2 tablespoons bacon drippings
3 tablespoons all-purpose flour
1 teaspoon sugar
1 teaspoon salt
  Breadcrumbs

Cook sausage slowly in heavy skillet until brown, crumbly, and well done. Add tomatoes and drained corn; simmer for 10 minutes. Sauté onion in bacon drippings; mix flour, sugar, and salt; blend with bacon drippings and onion. Add to sausage and vegetables; heat to boiling point. Spoon into 2-quart baking dish; top with breadcrumbs, slices of buttered bread cut in triangles, biscuit dough, or pastry. Bake at 425° for 20 minutes, or until topping is browned. Serve hot. Yield: 6 to 8 servings.

Favorite Pork and Dumplings

6 pork steaks or chops, bones removed
½ cup water
1 medium onion, thinly sliced
1½ to 3 cups water
  Dumplings

Brown meat in heavy, deep skillet. Add ½ cup water and sliced onion. Cover and simmer until meat is tender, about 45 to 50 minutes. Drain off excess fat and add additional water. Make Dumplings.

Dumplings

¾ cup milk
1½ cups instant-blending, self-rising flour

Add milk to flour and stir only until blended. Drop by spoonfuls onto hot meat (not in the liquid). Cook for 10 minutes, uncovered, then cover skillet and cook 10 minutes longer. Liquid can be thickened for gravy or served without the thickening. Yield: 6 servings.

Pork Hock Dinner

4 pork hocks
  Hot water
2 teaspoons salt
4 medium carrots
4 medium onions
4 medium potatoes
1 small head cabbage
  Salt
  Pepper
  Paprika

Wash hocks and place in Dutch oven or large, deep pan. Cover with hot water, add 2 teaspoons salt (if fresh hocks are used), and simmer, covered, until meat is nearly tender (about 1½ hours). Add whole carrots, peeled onions, and pared potatoes, cut in half. Cover and cook for 15 minutes. Add cabbage, cut in wedges, and cook, covered, for 15 minutes longer, or until vegetables are tender. Sprinkle vegetables with salt, pepper, and paprika. Yield: 4 servings.

Roast Pork with Apples And Potatoes

1 (3-pound) boned pork loin
2 to 3 teaspoons salt
½ teaspoon pepper
½ teaspoon thyme
½ teaspoon rosemary
  Pinch allspice
½ clove garlic, mashed
4 to 8 small potatoes
2 tart apples

Remove most of fat from roast. Combine salt and spices and rub over surface of roast. Cover and refrigerate for 12 hours before roasting. Wipe off seasonings. Roll and tie roast. Bake at 325° for about 35 to 40 minutes per pound, or until meat thermometer registers 185°. Add a small amount of hot water to the pan juices and baste from time to time.

Peel potatoes and slice lengthwise; add to roast when roast is about half-cooked. Fifteen minutes later add the apples which have been peeled and quartered. Skim fat from juices; serve juices with roast. Yield: 8 servings.

Fried Sausage

To cook bulk sausage, mold cakes about ½ inch thick and fry. In an uncovered pan, cook the cakes slowly and thoroughly until brown and crisp on both sides. Remove the cakes, drain on paper to remove excess fat, and serve hot.

Before cooking link or cased sausage, prick the casing in several places with a fork. Lay the pieces in a cold skillet, add 1 or 2 tablespoons water, cover and steam for a few minutes. Remove lid and finish cooking at moderate heat until thoroughly done, turning frequently.

Maryland Stuffed Ham

Cover an 8- to 10-pound ham with cold water and bring to a boil. Turn ham and boil for 10 minutes. Skin ham and set aside to cool.

Scald 5 pounds mixed kale and watercress. Chop 1 dozen spring onions, 1 large bunch parsley, and 1 entire stalk celery. Mix scalded greens, chopped greens, and add 2 teaspoons salt, ½ teaspoon pepper, 2 teaspoons celery seed, and 2 teaspoons mustard seed.

With a wide knife, gash ham deeply with blade held the long way of ham (not over 12 gashes for whole ham). Stuff gashes well with mixed greens and seasonings. Place ham in prepared cloth sack and pack extra greens around it. Sew tightly, cover with water, and boil for 3 hours, then cool in kettle. When quite cold, remove and drain. Take off sack and place ham on platter with extra stuffing all over it. Slice and serve cold. Yield: 10 to 12 servings.

Boiled Ham

To boil an old Kentucky or Virginia ham, put washed ham into a large boiler and completely cover with boiling water. Simmer until tender, but do not boil. Cook for 25 to 30 minutes to the pound. When ham is about half-done, add 1 cup vinegar and 1 cup brown sugar. Let ham remain in liquid until it is cold.

Mississippi Stuffed Ham And Dressing

Bake ham half-done. Skin, remove excessive fat (½ inch). Turn over and insert small vegetable knife at the hock and split, following the bone carefully. Cut bone out of the meat, leaving as little meat on it as possible. When bone is removed, fill cavity with a highly seasoned Dressing made of bread-crumbs, pressing it well into all cut places. Pour in a little melted butter.

Sew up the ham with a cord. Make enough Dressing to cover entire ham (½ inch). Moisten with juice of ham, and wrap in cheesecloth. Bake at 275°. Leave cheesecloth on until ham is cold.

Dressing

1 pound breadcrumbs
3 cups crumbled cornbread
1 teaspoon ground cloves
1 teaspoon ground allspice
1 teaspoon ground ginger
1 teaspoon ground mace
1 teaspoon onion salt
1 teaspoon garlic salt
1 teaspoon black pepper
½ cup molasses
2 tablespoons mustard
3 eggs, well beaten

Mix the crumbs, cornbread, and all spices well. Add molasses, mustard, and eggs. Moisten with juice of ham, and fill cavity.

Baked Country Ham

1 (10-pound) country-cured ham
1 cup ginger ale
1 cup brown sugar or ½ cup molasses
4 tablespoons all-purpose flour
1 tablespoon dry mustard
2 tablespoons water
  Whole cloves

Wash ham. Cover with boiling water and boil for 10 minutes. Then simmer for 3 hours. Remove skin, place in roaster, fat-side up. Bake at 325° for 1½ hours, basting frequently with a mixture of ginger ale and ham stock. Remove from oven. Cover with a paste made of brown sugar or molasses, flour, mustard, and water. Dot with cloves. Return to oven in uncovered roaster and bake for 30 minutes. Yield: 10 to 12 servings.

Fried Ham with Red-Eye Gravy

Slice ham about ¼ to ½ inch thick. Cut gashes in fat to keep ham from curling. Place slices in a heavy skillet and cook slowly. Turn several times, and cook until ham is brown. Remove from pan and keep warm. To the drippings in the skillet, add about ½ cup hot water; cook until gravy turns red. A little strong coffee might be added to deepen the color. Serve hot with fried ham and biscuits.

Broiled Ham Slice

Have ham slice cut ¾ to 1 inch thick. Score fat around edge of ham to prevent curling. Place on broiler rack in broiler pan. When inserting broiler pan in oven, allow 2 inches between surface of meat and heat. When brown, turn and brown second side. Broil 8 to 10 minutes on each side. Yield: 4 to 6 servings.

Roasting Chart
For Whole Chickens

Approximate Weight (Pounds)	Oven Temperature (Degrees)	Approximate Cooking Time (Hours)
3½ to 4	350	2 to 2¾
4 to 5	350	2½ to 3
over 5	325	3 to 3½

Chicken Pie Superb

  1 (4- to 5-pound) chicken
  1 carrot, diced
  1 onion, diced
  1 stalk celery, chopped
  1 sprig parsley, chopped
  1 teaspoon rosemary
  ½ teaspoon salt
  ⅛ teaspoon pepper
  5 tablespoons all-purpose flour
1½ cups chicken stock
  1 cup cream
  1 teaspoon salt
  ¼ teaspoon pepper
  ¼ pound butter or margarine
  1 (4-ounce) can mushroom slices
    Pastry

Clean and disjoint chicken. Place on rack in container half-filled with hot water. Add carrot, onion, celery, parsley, rosemary, ½ teaspoon salt, and pepper. Partly cover with a lid and simmer for 3 to 4 hours or until tender, turning occasionally. Cool chicken in broth, breast-side down. Skim off excess fat from stock.

Make a sauce by blending flour with ¼ cup of the strained stock in a saucepan. Stir in slowly the remaining stock and cream. Cook until thick, stirring constantly to avoid lumps. Season with salt and pepper. Place the chicken in a baking dish. Add the sauce. Dot butter or margarine over sauce and chicken. Add mushrooms. Cover sauce and chicken with a pastry, ⅓ inch thick.

Press pastry against sides of dish and cut gashes across the top. Bake at 425° for 12 to 15 minutes. Yield: 6 servings.

Chicken and Rolled Dumplings

Disjoint chicken, barely cover with water, and add 1½ teaspoons salt. Simmer until meat is tender, 2 to 4 hours, depending on age and size of chicken. Add Dumplings.

Rolled Dumplings

  2 cups all-purpose flour
  2 teaspoons baking powder
  1 teaspoon salt
  ⅓ cup shortening
  ½ cup milk

Combine flour, baking powder, and salt. Cut in shortening. Add milk to make a stiff dough. Roll out to about ⅛-inch thickness, and cut into 1-inch squares, 1- to 1½-inch strips, or diamonds. Sprinkle lightly with flour and drop into boiling chicken stock. Cover closely and boil gently for 8 to 10 minutes. Yield: 6 to 8 servings.

Fried Chicken

  1 (1½- to 2½-pound) fryer
  1 cup all-purpose flour
  ½ teaspoon salt
  ¼ teaspoon fresh ground pepper
    Shortening

Dress and disjoint fryer. Chill overnight. Combine flour, salt, and pepper. Put flour mixture into paper bag and drop in several pieces of chicken at a time. Shake bag to coat chicken with flour. Melt 1½ to 2 inches shortening in a large, hot frying pan. When all chicken is in, cover for 5 to 7 minutes. Uncover, and turn chicken when underside is golden brown. Cover again for 5 to 10 minutes; then remove top, and cook until other side is brown. Reduce heat, cover, and cook 20 to 25 minutes longer. Turn chicken only once. Yield: 4 servings.

Variations

Add one or more of the following to the flour — ¼ teaspoon paprika, monosodium glutamate, chili powder, or curry powder. Some cooks insist that chicken be left in sweet milk for an hour or so (this milk may be used later in gravy). Others dip the pieces of chicken into buttermilk before coating with flour.

Roast Chicken

Rub cavity lightly with salt. Place enough dressing in neck end to fill. Fasten neck skin down to back with skewer. Stuff body cavity with dressing. Cover chicken with a tent of aluminum foil or a cloth dipped in melted fat.

Place bird in a shallow pan on a rack on its side, or place bird breast down in V-shaped rack and leave in this position throughout the roasting. Roast at 325° or 350° until tender, turning bird on other side when half-done. Baste with drippings occasionally.

Chicken Supreme

  4 chicken breasts, cut in half
¼ pound butter or margarine
¼ cup all-purpose flour
½ teaspoon salt
  1 teaspoon paprika
  8 slices ham (country cured preferred)
  2 cups diced celery
  1 cup orange juice
  1 cup commercial sour cream

Lightly salt chicken breasts. Melt butter or margarine. Mix flour, salt, and

paprika in bag. Add chicken and shake to coat each piece evenly. Brown lightly in butter or margarine.

Grease an 8- x 12-inch baking dish. Place slices of ham in dish, cover with diced celery. Place browned chicken breasts, skin-side up, on the ham slices. Add flour left in bag to melted butter or margarine; blend well, then add orange juice. Remove from heat and add sour cream. Pour this gravy over chicken. Cover baking dish and bake at 350° for 1 hour and 15 minutes. Yield: 4 servings.

Country Captain

  2 large hens
  4 medium green peppers
  2 small onions
  2 cloves garlic
  2 tablespoons butter or margarine
  3 teaspoons curry powder
  2 teaspoons thyme
    Salt and pepper to taste
  3 (4-ounce) can mushrooms
½ pound blanched almonds
½ pound currants or raisins
    Cooked rice

Cut up chicken and steam until tender. While chicken is steaming, cut up peppers, onions, garlic, and sauté in a frying pan until slightly brown, not done. Add to this, curry powder, thyme, salt, pepper, tomatoes, and mushrooms. When this is well blended, add cooked chicken and half of blanched and toasted almonds, and half of raisins; cook together for 1 hour. (Do not thicken gravy.) When ready to serve, pour mixture over cooked rice, or place rice around it, and sprinkle remaining almonds and raisins over the whole. Yield: 6 to 8 servings.

Roasting Chart For Lamb

Roasting at 300° to 325°

Cut	Approximate Weight (Pounds)	Meat Thermometer Reading (Degrees)	Approximate Cooking Time (Minutes Per Pound)
Leg	5 to 8	175-180	30 to 35
Boneless Leg	3 to 5	175-180	35 to 40
Crown Roast	4 to 6	175-180	40 to 45
Rib (Rack)	4 to 5	175-180	40 to 45
Shoulder (bone-in)	4 to 6	175-180	30 to 35
Shoulder (cushion-style)	3 to 5	175-180	30 to 35
Shoulder (rolled)	3 to 5	175-180	40 to 45

Roast Lamb

Wipe leg of lamb with a clean, damp cloth. Season with salt and pepper. Place roast, fat side up, on a rack in an open roasting pan. Do not add water; do not cover; and do not baste. Roast at 325°. To determine doneness accurately, use a meat thermometer. For medium done, roast for 30 to 35 minutes per pound, or until meat thermometer registers 175°. For well done, roast for 35 to 40 minutes per pound, or until meat thermometer registers 182°.

Glorified Lamb Chops

1 teaspoon dry mustard
2 teaspoons butter or margarine
6 thick lamb chops
2 cups buttered cracker crumbs
2 teaspoons salt
⅛ teaspoon pepper

Mix mustard and butter or margarine until well blended, and spread over each lamb chop. Roll the chops in buttered cracker crumbs, season with salt and pepper, and broil until tender. Yield: 6 servings.

Roasting Chart For Whole Turkeys

Approximate Weight (Pounds)	Oven Temperature (Degrees)	Approximate Cooking Time (Hours)
4 to 8	325	3 to 4
8 to 12	325	4 to 4½
12 to 16	325	4½ to 5
16 to 20	325	5½ to 7
20 to 24	325	7 to 8½

Roast Turkey

Start preparing the stuffing a day or so ahead of time if you like, but refrigerate dry ingredients and broth separately until time to use the dressing. Do not stuff the turkey until time to roast it.

For each generous serving of roasted whole turkey, allow ¾ to 1 pound of ready-to-cook weight for birds weighing less than 12 pounds; ½ to ¾ pound for birds weighing 12 pounds and over. Clean bird thoroughly. Salt inside of bird. Fill the neck cavity loosely with dressing. Fold the neck skin to back, fastening to backbone with a poultry pin. Fold wingtip over neck skin. Spoon the dressing into body cavity, shaking the bird to settle dressing. Do not pack it. Place skewers across opening and lace shut with cord. Tie drumsticks securely to tail. Brush skin with soft fat.

Cover the turkey with a tent of aluminum foil or a piece of thin cloth moistened with fat. Baste the turkey with pan drippings or melted fat several times during roasting. When the roasting is about half-done, cut the string or skin to release the legs; the bird cooks better and looks better.

Turkey is done when the leg joints move easily and the flesh on the legs is soft and pliable when pressed with the fingers. When a meat thermometer is used, it should register 185° placed in the center of the inside thigh muscle or in the center of the thickest meaty part.

Use the chart to determine how long to roast turkey. It gives the approximate time required to cook chilled turkeys of various weights. Stuffed turkeys require approximately 5 minutes per pound more time.

Roast Cornish Game Hen

1 *individual-size Cornish hen*
4 *tablespoons melted butter or margarine*
  Herb Gravy

Place bird, breast-side down, in baking pan which has a tight-fitting cover.

Brush back with butter or margarine. Roast uncovered at 400° until hen begins to brown, about 20 minutes. Reduce heat to 350°. Cover closely and roast until thoroughly tender — the entire time will be about 1 hour — but hen must be tested for tenderness. Use drippings to make Herb Gravy. Yield: 1 to 2 servings.

Herb Gravy

¼ *cup drippings*
½ *cup instant nonfat dry milk powder*
2 *tablespoons all-purpose flour*
½ *teaspoon whole basil, crushed*
¼ *teaspoon powdered marjoram*
1½ *cups water*

Pour drippings into roasting pan or saucepan. In another container, sprinkle dry milk powder, flour, and seasonings over water, beat until just blended. Pour into drippings. Blend well, cook over low heat, stirring constantly until thickened. Serve hot over Cornish Game Hen.

Favorite Bread Dressing

1 *cup minced onion*
1 *quart diced celery*
1 *cup shortening*
1 *tablespoon salt*
½ *teaspoon pepper*
2 *teaspoons poultry seasoning*
4 *quarts breadcrumbs*
1½ *to 2 cups broth or water*

Cook onion and celery in shortening over low heat until onion is soft but not browned, stirring occasionally. Meanwhile blend seasonings with bread, which has been crumbled. Add the onion, celery, and fat and blend. Pour the broth gradually over surface, stirring lightly. Add more seasoning as desired. Yield: Dressing for a 14- to 18-pound turkey.

Company Beef Casserole

1 pound ground beef
2 tablespoons shortening
1 medium onion, chopped
2 cups canned tomatoes
1 tablespoon catsup
1 tablespoon steak sauce
¼ cup chopped green pepper
2 tablespoons chopped parsley
1 (5-ounce) package elbow macaroni
  Salt and pepper
1 (10½-ounce) can cream of
  mushroom soup
1 cup shredded Cheddar cheese

Brown ground beef in shortening in heavy skillet until all red color disappears. Add onion, tomatoes, catsup, steak sauce, green pepper, and parsley. Simmer for 30 minutes. Cook macaroni according to package directions. Combine macaroni and ground beef mixture in a 2-quart baking dish. Season to taste. Gently spoon mushroom soup into mixture. Mix lightly, lifting from the bottom. Sprinkle shredded cheese over the top. Bake at 350° for 30 minutes, or until top is bubbly and browned. Yield: 6 servings.

Beef-Macaroni Casserole

1½ cups cut macaroni
 2 teaspoons shortening
½ cup chopped onion
 1 pound ground beef
 1 teaspoon salt
 1 teaspoon steak sauce
¼ teaspoon pepper
½ cup catsup
1½ cups shredded cheese
 1 egg
1½ cups milk
½ cup catsup

Cook macaroni according to package directions. Drain, and place in a large mixing bowl. Place shortening in a skillet and cook the chopped onion until browned. Add ground beef and cook until all color is removed. Drain off excess fat. Add salt, steak sauce, pepper, and ½ cup catsup. Mix the meat and macaroni and let cool. When mixture is cool, add shredded cheese and mix well. Place mixture in two 1-quart casserole dishes.

To bake: Mix together egg, milk, and ½ cup catsup and additional shredded cheese, if desired. Pour over the casserole mixture and bake in a covered casserole dish at 350° about 25 to 30 minutes, or until it heats through and starts to bubble. Yield: 8 servings.

Note: This is an excellent dish to make ahead of time and freeze.

Spanish Casserole

1 large onion, chopped
1 large green pepper, chopped
  Shortening
1 pound ground beef
2 cups corn
1 (10½-ounce) can condensed
  tomato soup
2 (3-ounce) cans mushroom slices
1 teaspoon chili powder
1 (5-ounce) package noodles
½ cup shredded cheese

Sauté the onion and green pepper in small amount of shortening. Add ground beef and brown. Then add corn, soup, mushrooms, and chili powder. Cook the noodles for 5 minutes. Drain and add to meat mixture. Put in a 2-quart baking dish and bake at 350° for 30 minutes. Yield: 8 servings.

Corned Beef Casserole

1 (8-ounce) package macaroni
1 (10½-ounce) can cream of chicken
   soup
1 (12-ounce) can corned beef, cut into
   small pieces
1 cup milk
¼ pound Cheddar cheese, shredded
1 small onion, chopped
   Buttered breadcrumbs

Cook macaroni according to package
directions. Drain. Combine with soup,
corned beef, milk, cheese, and onion.
Put into a greased 1½-quart casserole
dish and top with breadcrumbs. Bake at
350° about 30 minutes or until crumbs
are browned. Yield: 6 to 8 servings.

Ranch Casserole

1½ pounds ground beef
 2 tablespoons shortening
 1 teaspoon salt
 1 package onion soup mix
½ cup water
 1 cup catsup
 2 tablespoons prepared mustard
 2 tablespoons vinegar
½ cup piccalilli relish

Sauté meat in shortening. Add other
ingredients and cook in covered skillet
about 30 minutes, or bake in covered
casserole at 325° for 30 to 40 minutes.
Serve over rice or on buns. Yield: 6 to
8 servings.

Macaroni and Cheese

 2 tablespoons butter or margarine
 2 tablespoons all-purpose flour
1½ cups milk
 2 eggs
 1 cup shredded Cheddar cheese
½ teaspoon Worcestershire sauce
 3 drops Tabasco sauce
1½ cups cooked macaroni

Melt butter or margarine in top of double boiler; add flour, and stir until well
blended. Reserve 2 tablespoons of the
milk to mix with eggs. Pour remaining
milk gradually into butter-flour mixture, stirring constantly. Cook until
smooth. Pour gradually into slightly
beaten eggs mixed with milk. Add
cheese, and stir until melted. Add
Worcestershire sauce and Tabasco and
pour over macaroni in a 1½-quart baking dish. Bake at 350° for 35 minutes.
Yield: 6 servings.

Simply Delicious
Skillet Dinner

 1 tablespoon shortening
½ pound ground beef
 1 medium onion, chopped
 1 small clove garlic, minced
 2 tablespoons minced parsley
 1 (6-ounce) can tomato paste
2¼ cups water
 1 teaspoon sugar
 1 teaspoon salt
   Dash pepper
 1 (5-ounce) package noodles
   Parmesan cheese

Melt shortening in heavy skillet; add
ground beef, onion, garlic, and parsley.
Brown lightly. Combine tomato paste
with water, sugar, salt, and pepper,
mixing until smooth. Add to meat mixture, mixing well. Cover, reduce heat,
and simmer for 10 minutes. Add
noodles, cover, and cook until noodles are
tender, stirring occasionally. Serve
with grated Parmesan cheese. Yield:
4 servings.

Grits Casserole

1 cup regular grits
3 cups boiling water
½ teaspoon salt
½ stick butter or margarine
4 eggs
1 cup milk
¼ cup shredded Cheddar cheese

Pour the grits into boiling water to which salt has been added. Mix well, and cook until thickened. Add the butter or margarine, beaten eggs, milk, and cheese. Stir thoroughly and place in a greased 2-quart casserole. Bake at 350° about 30 minutes. Yield: 4 to 6 servings.

Mexican Rice Casserole

4 slices bacon and drippings
½ cup chopped onion
½ cup chopped green pepper
1 cup uncooked regular rice
1 pound ground beef
1 small clove garlic
1¾ cups water
1 (8-ounce) can tomato sauce
¾ cup raisins
2 teaspoons salt
1 tablespoon chili powder
2½ cups shredded cheese

Fry bacon until crisp. Remove from pan and drain. Add onion and pepper to drippings and cook until tender. Add rice and cook until golden. Stir in beef and garlic; cook until meat is almost done. Stir in water, tomato sauce, raisins, and seasonings. Heat to boiling. Reduce heat, cover and simmer for 20 minutes. Spoon half of mixture into a greased 2-quart casserole. Sprinkle with half of cheese and half of crumbled bacon. Add remainder of meat mixture and top with remaining cheese and bacon. Bake at 450° about 15 minutes or until cheese is bubbly. Yield: 8 servings.

Hot Sausage Pie

1 pound pork sausage
2 cups canned tomatoes
2 cups whole-kernel corn
2 tablespoons minced onion
2 tablespoons bacon drippings
3 tablespoons all-purpose flour
1 teaspoon sugar
1 teaspoon salt
Buttered breadcrumbs

Cook sausage slowly in skillet until brown, crumbly, and well done. Add tomatoes and drained corn; simmer for 10 minutes. Sauté onion in bacon drippings; mix flour, sugar, and salt; blend with bacon drippings and onion. Add to sausage and vegetables and heat to boiling point. Spoon into 2-quart baking dish; top with buttered breadcrumbs and bake at 425° for 20 minutes, or until topping is browned. Serve hot. Yield: 6 to 8 servings.

Skillet Sausage and Sweets

1 (10½-ounce) can condensed consommé
1 tablespoon cornstarch
2 tablespoons brown sugar
1 tablespoon orange juice
1 teaspoon grated lemon rind
1 (1-pound, 7-ounce) can sweet potatoes, drained
1 pound sausage links, cooked
8 apple slices (about 1 medium cooking apple)
Chopped pecans (optional)

Gradually blend consommé into cornstarch; add sugar, juice, and lemon rind. Heat; stir until thickened. Add potatoes, sausage, and apple slices. Cook over low heat about 20 minutes, spooning glaze over ingredients. Garnish with pecans, if desired. Yield: 4 servings.

Asparagus Casserole

2 tablespoons butter or margarine
2 tablespoons all-purpose flour
2 tablespoons asparagus liquid
1 cup cream
½ teaspoon salt
½ teaspoon pepper
   Dash paprika
½ cup shredded cheese
1 (3-ounce) can mushrooms
2 (14½-ounce) cans asparagus
   Cracker crumbs

Melt butter or margarine and gradually add flour, stirring constantly. Add asparagus liquid, and mix well. Add cream, stirring constantly until thick. Season with salt, pepper, and paprika. Add cheese, and stir until melted. Add mushrooms. Line bottom of 1½-quart casserole with one can of the drained asparagus. Cover with sauce. Add second can of asparagus and cracker crumbs. Bake at 350° for about 25 minutes. Yield: 6 servings.

Eggplant Casserole

2 cups diced eggplant
½ cup diced celery
¼ cup chopped onion
1 egg, slightly beaten
⅓ cup milk or cream
2 tablespoons butter or margarine
1 cup breadcrumbs
½ cup shredded cheese

Peel, dice, and measure eggplant. Cook until tender in a small amount of boiling salted water. Sauté celery and onion until tender. Drain eggplant; add to celery and onions, and sauté slightly. Remove from heat, and add beaten egg and milk or cream. Pour in a 1-quart baking dish. Dot with butter or margarine, sprinkle with breadcrumbs, and cover with shredded cheese. Bake at 350° for 30 minutes. Yield: 6 servings.

Note: You may add ½ to 1 cup of finely diced ham, roast, or other leftover meat to this recipe.

Squash Casserole

1½ pounds yellow squash
1 small onion, minced
1 tablespoon minced parsley
1 egg, slightly beaten
¼ cup milk
½ cup cottage cheese, sieved
½ teaspoon salt
½ teaspoon pepper
1 teaspoon sugar
¼ cup finely chopped pecans

Parboil squash, mash, and add all other ingredients except nuts. Place in 1-quart casserole, and sprinkle pecans over the top. Bake at 350° about 30 to 45 minutes, or until top is browned. Yield: 6 to 8 servings.

Cheese Pudding

8 slices white bread
⅓ cup butter or margarine
2 cups shredded cheese
3 cups milk
4 eggs
1⅓ teaspoons salt
⅓ teaspoon dry mustard

Spread the bread with butter or margarine and cut each slice into four pieces. Alternate layers of cheese and bread in greased, flat baking dish so that cheese is on top. Combine milk, eggs, salt, and mustard. Pour mixture over cheese and bread. Let stand in refrigerator overnight. Bake at 325° for about 40 minutes. Yield: 8 servings.

Fried Corn

8 ears fresh corn
½ cup milk
½ teaspoon salt
¼ teaspoon pepper
4 tablespoons butter or margarine
2 eggs, beaten

Cut corn from cob and add milk, salt, and pepper. Put butter or margarine in heavy skillet. When skillet is hot, add corn. Cook until tender, stirring occasionally. Just before ready to take up, add beaten eggs and blend in well. Serve hot. Yield: 6 servings.

Corn Pudding

2 cups fresh corn, cut from cob
1 cup milk
2 tablespoons butter or margarine
2 tablespoons all-purpose flour
1 teaspoon salt
1 tablespoon sugar
   Red or white pepper to taste
3 eggs

Cut corn from cob, or use leftover stewed corn. Add milk, butter or margarine, flour, and seasonings. Beat eggs together until light; add to the mixture. Pour into a buttered 1-quart baking dish, and bake at 350° for 1 hour, or until firm like a custard. Preferred method: Place dish with pudding in a pan of boiling water for better custard-like texture. Bake at 350° for 1 hour and 15 minutes, or until custard is set. Yield: 4 to 6 servings.

Fried Okra

2 pounds fresh okra
½ teaspoon salt
⅛ teaspoon pepper
½ cup cornmeal
4 tablespoons bacon drippings or salad oil

Wash okra well; drain. Larger pods of okra may need to be boiled in salted water until tender. Cut off tip and stem ends; slice okra across in ¼-inch rounds. Season slices with salt and pepper; roll in cornmeal. Sauté well coated okra in hot bacon drippings or salad oil until tender and golden brown on both sides. Yield: 8 servings.

Buttered Okra

1   pound fresh okra
1½ cups boiling water
1   teaspoon salt
2   tablespoons butter or margarine
     Pepper

Wash okra, but do not cut off stems. Add okra to boiling salted water. Cover, bring back to boiling and boil for 3 to 5 minutes. Remove from heat; drain. Add butter or margarine, and white or black pepper as desired. Yield: 4 servings.

Fried Green Tomatoes

4 large, firm, green tomatoes
½ cup all-purpose flour or cornmeal
1 teaspoon salt
¼ teaspoon pepper
   Bacon drippings or shortening

Cut tomatoes in ¼-inch slices. Mix flour or cornmeal with salt and pepper. Coat tomatoes with this mixture. Place in heavy skillet containing hot bacon drippings or shortening. Fry slowly until brown, turning once. Yield: 6 servings.

French Fried Onion Rings

4 large onions, peeled
⅔ cup milk
½ cup all-purpose flour
   Shortening for frying

Cut cleaned onions into ¼-inch slices and separate into rings. Soak onion rings in milk for 10 to 15 minutes. Dredge rings in flour, then fry in deep fat heated to 365°, a few at a time, until well browned (about 2 to 3 minutes). Drain on paper toweling. Season and serve immediately. Yield: 4 to 6 servings.

Buttered Spinach

1½ pounds fresh spinach
   Boiling water
½ teaspoon salt
1 tablespoon butter or margarine

Remove roots and discolored leaves. Wash at least five times to remove all sand. Lift out of water into another pan; do not bruise. Place spinach in large saucepan and add ½ inch boiling water. Cook uncovered for first few minutes of cooking. Turn with fork until all leaves are wilted. Cover and cook for 8 to 10 minutes. Drain, and add salt and butter or margarine. Yield: 4 servings.

Stuffed Green Peppers

8 to 10 green peppers, fresh or frozen
1 cup uncooked regular rice
1 tablespoon shortening
1 pound ground beef
¼ cup chopped onion
¼ cup chopped green pepper
1½ teaspoons salt
½ teaspoon black pepper, if desired

Cut stem ends from peppers and remove seed. Put peppers into boiling water and cook for 2 or 3 minutes. Remove from water and drain. Cook rice as directed on package. Melt shortening in heavy skillet; add ground beef, onion, chopped pepper, salt and black pepper. Brown, add to rice, and mix. Stuff peppers with mixture. Place in baking dish and bake at 350° for 30 minutes. Yield: 8 to 10 servings.

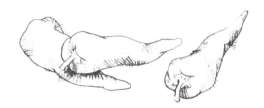

Fresh Turnip, Mustard, or Collard Greens

1 large bunch greens (about 2 to 2½ pounds)
¼ pound salt pork, diced
   About ½ cup boiling water
   Salt to taste

Check leaves of fresh greens carefully; remove pulpy stems and discolored spots on leaves. Wash thoroughly in several changes of warm water; add a little salt to the last water. Put greens into colander to drain.

Cook diced salt pork for about 10 minutes in boiling water in covered saucepan. Add washed greens a few at a time, cover pot, and cook slowly until greens are tender. Do not overcook. Add additional salt, if needed.

An alternate method is to wash greens carefully and put into large cooking pot with only the water that clings to leaves. Chopped turnip roots may be added when the greens are almost done. Add salt and bacon drippings after greens have cooked tender. Serve with vinegar or hot pepper sauce.

Creole String Beans

    4 cups canned or frozen string beans
    1 onion, sliced
    2 cups canned tomatoes
    1 teaspoon dried mixed herbs
    ½ cup salad oil
    6 strips bacon

Chop string beans and cook in salted water until tender. Add onion rings, canned tomatoes, herbs, salad oil, and bacon, cut in 1-inch strips. Simmer for 20 to 25 minutes, and serve hot. Yield: 6 servings.

Red Beans and Rice

    ½ cup chopped onions
    2 tablespoons butter or margarine
    1⅓ cups packaged precooked rice
    1 teaspoon salt
    ⅛ teaspoon pepper
    2 cups liquid (bean liquid plus
       tomato juice)
    2 cups drained red kidney beans
    ½ cup shredded sharp cheese

Sauté onions in the butter or margarine in saucepan over medium heat until tender, but not brown. Stir occasionally. Add precooked rice, salt, pepper, and liquid. Bring to a boil uncovered. Cover, and simmer gently for 3 minutes. Add beans to rice. Serve with shredded sharp cheese on top. Yield: 4 to 6 servings.

Stuffed Eggplant

    2 small eggplants
    ¼ cup diced green pepper
    ¼ cup diced onion
    ¼ cup diced celery
    1 tablespoon vegetable oil
    1 (10½-ounce) can condensed
       tomato soup
    1 cup cooked regular rice
    ½ teaspoon salt
       Dash pepper
       Dash thyme
    1½ cups cracker crumbs

Cut eggplants in half lengthwise and simmer in salted boiling water until almost tender (about 10 minutes). Brown the green pepper, onion, and celery in vegetable oil. Combine the soup, rice, salt, pepper, and thyme. Scoop out center of eggplants; leave ½ inch of pulp around edges (save pulp scooped out of eggplants and add to spaghetti sauce another day). Sprinkle 2 tablespoons cracker crumbs over bottom of each shell. Fill with rice mixture. Spread remaining crumbs over top; dot with butter or margarine. Bake at 375° for about 30 minutes. Yield: 4 servings.

Green Beans with Mushrooms

    4 cups cooked green beans
    1 (4-ounce) can mushrooms
    3 tablespoons butter or margarine

Drain bean and mushroom liquid into saucepan. Boil liquid rapidly until reduced to about ½ cup. Add drained beans, mushrooms, and butter or margarine; heat to serve. Yield: 6 to 8 servings.

Harvard Beets

    ½ cup sugar
    2 teaspoons cornstarch
    ½ cup vinegar
    12 small cooked beets or
       1 (16-ounce) can, drained
    2 tablespoons butter

Mix sugar, cornstarch, and vinegar together. Stir over low heat until thickened. Add butter and pour over prepared beets in saucepan and let stand on back of range for 30 minutes. If not warm enough, heat before serving. Yield: 4 servings.

Dried Butterbeans

Soak dried butterbeans overnight in soft water to cover. Drain; cook until tender in fresh boiling salted water with a slice of diced salt pork.

Five-Minute Cabbage

3 cups milk
8 cups chopped cabbage
3 tablespoons all-purpose flour
½ teaspoon salt
3 tablespoons bacon drippings

Heat milk to simmering. Add cabbage, and simmer for 2 minutes. Mix flour, salt, and bacon drippings. Add ½ cup of the hot milk to the flour mixture, and blend. Stir this into the cabbage and cook 3 minutes longer, stirring constantly. Serve hot. Yield: 8 servings.

Stuffed Whole Cabbage

1 (2-pound) head cabbage
  Boiling water to cover cabbage
1 cup finely chopped luncheon meat
1 cup shredded American cheese
¼ cup finely chopped onion
½ cup soft breadcrumbs
1 tablespoon milk
½ teaspoon salt
¼ teaspoon black pepper
1½ cups diced fresh tomatoes
¾ cup boiling water
¾ teaspoon salt
¾ cup bread cubes
1½ tablespoons melted butter or
  margarine

Remove outer leaves from cabbage and save them for salad or soup. Place cabbage head in a saucepan with 1 teaspoon salt and enough boiling water to cover. Boil, uncovered, until almost tender, about 30 minutes. Remove from water. Drain well. Cut off top and carefully scoop out inside leaving a 1½-inch shell. Place cabbage in a deep casserole. Finely shred enough of the cabbage center to make 1 cup. Combine with luncheon meat, cheese, onion, ½ cup breadcrumbs, milk, and salt. Mix well and spoon into the cabbage shell.

Combine tomatoes, water, salt. Pour into casserole around cabbage. Cover with aluminum foil or casserole top. Bake at 350° for 1 hour. Remove from oven and sprinkle with ¾ cup bread cubes mixed with melted butter or margarine. Bake for 15 minutes or until cubes have browned. Serve with some of the tomato sauce spooned over each portion. Yield: 6 servings.

Black-Eyed Peas with Ham Hock

1 pound dry black-eyed peas
5 to 6 cups water
1 small ham hock
1 to 3 teaspoons salt
1 large onion, whole

Put dry peas into a colander in sink partially filled with cold water or wash under cold running water; wash well and remove faulty peas. Drain and put into a heavy 6- to 8-quart kettle. Cover and soak for 12 hours or overnight.

The next day, add ham hock to kettle (add more water if water does not cover peas) and bring to a boil. Reduce heat and add 1 teaspoon or more salt (it is better to start with a smaller amount if salty ham hock is used). Add whole onion. Cover kettle and simmer for about 1 hour or until peas are tender. To avoid excessive breaking of peas, do not stir during cooking. Add more salt if needed. Yield: 6 servings.

Fresh Black-Eyed Peas

¼ pound thinly sliced fat pork
   Boiling water
4 cups shelled, washed, fresh
   black-eyed peas
1 teaspoon salt
¼ teaspoon black pepper
¼ teaspoon cayenne pepper
1 whole medium onion

Cover sliced pork with boiling water; cover pan and boil for 15 minutes. Add peas, salt, pepper, and onion; add enough water to cover peas. Cover pan and cook for about 45 minutes, or until peas are tender. Add more seasoning to taste. Yield: 6 to 8 servings.

Hopping John

1 cup black-eyed peas
1 medium ham hock
1 medium onion, diced
2 stalks celery, chopped
1 small bay leaf
2 to 3 cups water
½ teaspoon salt
¼ teaspoon pepper
1 cup uncooked regular rice

Put peas, ham hock, onion, celery, and bay leaf in saucepan and add water and seasoning. Simmer, covered, until peas are tender. Cook rice. Combine peas, rice, ham, and liquid from peas. Simmer. Yield: 8 servings.

Creamed Potatoes

2 cups diced, raw potatoes
   Salted water
2 tablespoons butter or margarine
1 cup hot milk or cream
   Salt and pepper

Cook potatoes in small amount of salted water until tender. Drain. Whip the potatoes until smooth and fluffy. Add butter or margarine, milk or cream, and blend well. Add salt and pepper to taste. Set over hot water until ready to serve. Yield: 4 to 6 servings.

Hash Browned Potatoes

2 cups diced, cooked potatoes
2 tablespoons finely chopped onion
4 teaspoons all-purpose flour
1½ teaspoons salt
   Pepper
2 tablespoons milk
2 to 3 tablespoons melted shortening

Combine potatoes and onion. Mix flour, salt, and pepper, and slowly blend in the milk. Combine with potato-onion mixture. Heat shortening in a heavy skillet. Add potatoes, and cook over medium heat until the under side is brown. Turn to brown the other side. Yield: 4 servings.

Baked Potatoes

Choose firm, smooth potatoes of the baking type. Scrub potatoes thoroughly and dry. If you like a crunchy crust, bake without any coating or covering. If you like the skin soft, rub with shortening or cover with aluminum foil. Bake at 425° for 40 to 60 minutes, depending on size. When potatoes are done, roll gently under the hand to make the inside mealy. Make a criss-cross slash on top and gently push up. Add salt, pepper, and butter.

Squash au Gratin

2 cups cooked squash
2 tablespoons butter or
   margarine, melted
   Salt and pepper
2 eggs, beaten
1 cup buttered breadcrumbs
⅓ cup shredded cheese

Combine squash, melted butter or margarine, seasonings, and beaten eggs. Alternate layers of squash, breadcrumbs, and cheese in 1-quart casserole; bake at 375° for 10 minutes. Yield: 4 servings.

Baked Squash

6 medium squash
½ medium onion, chopped
½ cup diced cooked ham
3 tablespoons butter or margarine
½ cup milk
1 egg
½ cup breadcrumbs
   Salt and pepper to taste

Cut squash in pieces and cook in small amount of water until tender. Drain thoroughly and mash. Add all other ingredients, mix, and bake in a 1-quart casserole at 325° for 30 minutes. Yield: 4 servings.

Sweet Potato Pudding

1 cup butter or margarine
1 cup sugar
6 egg yolks
2 teaspoons brandy flavoring
2 teaspoons sherry flavoring
1 teaspoon ground allspice
1 teaspoon ground cinnamon
1 teaspoon ground ginger
   Ground nutmeg to taste
1 lemon
2 cups cooked sweet potatoes
6 egg whites, stiffly beaten

Cream together the butter or margarine and sugar; add egg yolks and beat well. Add flavorings, spices, lemon juice, and grated lemon rind. Combine with the sieved or finely mashed sweet potatoes. Fold stiffly beaten egg whites into the potato mixture. Place in a 2-quart buttered baking dish and bake at 350° for 45 minutes. Yield: 6 servings.

Orange Candied Sweet Potatoes

6 medium sweet potatoes
1 cup orange juice
½ teaspoon grated orange rind
1 cup water
2 cups sugar
¼ cup butter or margarine
½ teaspoon salt

Peel and slice uncooked potatoes in ¼-inch slices; arrange in buttered 1½-quart baking dish. Make syrup of other ingredients and pour over potatoes. Cover and bake at 350° for about 30 minutes or until tender. Baste occasionally. Remove lid the last 10 minutes to brown. Yield: 6 servings.

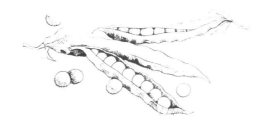

Candied Sweet Potatoes

3 large sweet potatoes
1 cup brown sugar
   Ground cinnamon
4 tablespoons melted butter
6 pieces orange peel
½ cup water

Boil whole potatoes until tender. Remove skins and slice thin. Put a layer of potatoes into buttered 1½-quart baking dish and sprinkle with sugar, cinnamon, and butter. Repeat until all potatoes are used. When dish is filled, sprinkle top with sugar, cinnamon, butter, and orange peel. Add water and bake at 350° about 30 minutes, or until brown and well candied. Yield: 4 servings.

Baking Powder Biscuits

2 cups all-purpose flour
3 teaspoons baking powder
1 teaspoon salt
¼ cup shortening
¾ cup milk

Combine the dry ingredients, and cut in the shortening. Add milk, stirring until all flour is moistened. Turn out on lightly floured board. Work the biscuits for about 20 seconds, then roll out to ½-inch thickness. Cut out biscuits and place on ungreased baking sheet. Bake at 450° for about 8 to 10 minutes. Yield: 12 (2-inch) biscuits.

Sourdough Biscuits

Starter

1 peeled, grated, medium potato
1 cup sugar
3 cups water
3 cups all-purpose flour

Combine all ingredients and let stand in gallon jar or crock, lightly covered with a cloth, for 3 days. After a cup of starter is taken out to make biscuits, add 1 cup water, ½ cup flour, and 1 tablespoon sugar to the starter so that there will be a supply for the next batch of biscuits.

Biscuits

1 cup starter
¼ cup melted shortening
½ teaspoon salt
    About 1 cup all-purpose flour

Mix all ingredients, adding enough flour to make dough easy to handle. Roll to about ½-inch thickness on floured board. Cut out and place on greased baking sheet. Bake at 425° for 20 minutes. Serve hot. Yield: 12 biscuits.

Country Cornbread

1½ cups cornmeal
¾ cup all-purpose flour
1 teaspoon salt
2½ teaspoons baking powder
2 eggs, beaten
1½ cups milk
6 tablespoons shortening

Combine cornmeal, flour, salt, and baking powder. Combine beaten eggs and milk and stir into cornmeal mixture. Mix well. Put shortening into a 10-inch skillet and put into preheated 400° oven. As soon as shortening is very hot, coat sides of skillet and stir remaining shortening into cornbread mixture. Spoon mixture into hot skillet and bake for about 20 to 25 minutes or until golden brown. Yield: 6 to 8 servings.

Buttermilk Biscuits

2 cups all-purpose flour
½ teaspoon soda
⅔ teaspoon salt
3 tablespoons shortening
¾ cup buttermilk

Combine dry ingredients. Cut in shortening. Add milk all at once. Knead lightly and roll out to ½-inch thickness. Cut out and place on ungreased baking sheet. Bake at 450° for 12 to 15 minutes. Yield: 12 (2-inch) biscuits.

Buttermilk Cornbread

1 cup cornmeal
4 tablespoons all-purpose flour
½ teaspoon soda
1 teaspoon salt
1 tablespoon melted shortening
1 egg
1 cup buttermilk

Sift together cornmeal, flour, soda, and salt. Melt shortening in pan in which cornbread is to be baked. Beat egg and add to buttermilk. Then pour this mixture into the sifted dry ingredients and stir only until well mixed. Add the melted shortening; stir well. Pour batter into hot, greased 10-inch pan. Bake at 425° for about 30 to 35 minutes or until brown. Yield: 6 servings.

Ham Biscuits

Use large, crusty biscuits. Split, and insert a generous slice of fried or baked ham. On the other hand, for a tea or a party nothing can surpass a tiny, crunchy biscuit with a filling of tasty minced ham, or slivers of baked ham.

Corn Pone

    1 tablespoon shortening
  ¾ cup boiling water
    1 cup cornmeal
    1 teaspoon salt

Melt shortening in pan or heavy 10-inch skillet in which pone is to be cooked. Pour boiling water over cornmeal and salt. Add melted shortening. Stir to blend well. As soon as mixture is cool enough to handle, divide into four equal portions. Form each into a pone about ¾-inch thick by patting between hands. Place in greased pan, and bake at 450° for about 50 minutes, or until a light crust is formed. Yield: 6 to 8 servings.

Crackling Bread

  ¼ cup all-purpose flour
1½ cups cornmeal
  ½ teaspoon soda
  ¼ teaspoon salt
    1 cup sour milk
    1 cup diced cracklings

Mix all dry ingredients. Add the milk, and stir in the cracklings. Form into oblong cakes and place in a greased 12-inch baking pan. Bake at 400° for about 30 minutes. Yield: 6 to 8 servings.

Hot Water Cornbread

    1 cup cornmeal
    1 cup boiling water
    1 teaspoon salt
    1 tablespoon shortening
    1 teaspoon sugar
    1 egg
1⅛ cups milk
    1 teaspoon baking powder

Heat a greased 10-inch heavy skillet in oven. Combine cornmeal, water, salt, shortening, and sugar. Stir until mixed. Beat egg and combine with milk. Mix, and stir gradually into cornmeal mixture. Beat in baking powder. Pour into hot, greased skillet. Bake at 425° for 20 minutes. Reduce heat to 350° and bake for 30 minutes, or until firm and light brown. Yield: 6 servings.

Hush Puppies with Onions

1¾ cups cornmeal
    4 tablespoons all-purpose flour
    1 teaspoon baking powder
    1 teaspoon salt
    6 tablespoons chopped onion
    1 egg, beaten
    2 cups boiling water

Combine dry ingredients. Add chopped onion and beaten egg. Pour boiling water over this mixture, stirring constantly until mixture is smooth. Add more water if necessary. Drop by spoonfuls into deep, hot fat. Yield: 8 to 10 servings.

Sweet Milk Cornbread

1 cup yellow cornmeal
1 cup sifted all-purpose flour
¼ cup sugar (optional)
½ teaspoon salt
3 teaspoons baking powder
1 egg
1 cup milk
¼ cup melted shortening

Sift together cornmeal, flour, sugar, salt, and baking powder. Beat egg, add milk, and combine with dry ingredients. Add shortening. Pour into hot, greased 10-inch skillet or pan, muffin pan, or corn stick pan. Bake at 375° to 400° for 25 to 30 minutes, or until golden brown. Yield: 6 servings.

Basic Pancakes

1½ cups sifted all-purpose flour
2 teaspoons baking powder
1 tablespoon sugar
1 teaspoon salt
1 egg, slightly beaten
1¼ cups milk
2 tablespoons melted butter or margarine

Combine dry ingredients. Break egg in a large mixing bowl and beat slightly. Stir in the milk and melted butter or margarine. Add sifted dry ingredients all at once; stir only until flour is moistened. Do not beat. Cook on greased, hot griddle. Yield: 8 servings.

Variations

Bacon Pancakes — Break 6 slices crisp, cooked bacon into small bits and add to batter.

Pecan Pancakes — Fold ½ cup chopped pecans into batter, or sprinkle pecans on batter in the griddle.

Cheese Pancakes — Add ½ cup coarsely shredded Cheddar cheese to the milk and egg mixture.

Buttermilk Waffles

2 cups sifted all-purpose flour
3 teaspoons baking powder
1 teaspoon soda
1 teaspoon salt
2 cups buttermilk
4 eggs, well beaten
½ cup melted butter or margarine

Heat waffle iron while mixing batter. Combine flour, baking powder, soda, and salt. Combine buttermilk and eggs and add to flour mixture. Beat until smooth. Stir in melted butter or margarine. Pour batter from a pitcher or cup onto waffle iron. Close waffle iron at once. Serve hot. Yield: 8 servings.

Banana-Nut Bread

½ cup shortening
1 cup sugar
2 eggs
1 cup mashed ripe bananas
¼ cup chopped nuts
2 cups all-purpose flour
1 teaspoon soda
¼ teaspoon salt

Cream shortening and sugar until light and fluffy. Add eggs and beat well. Stir in mashed bananas and mix well. Stir in nuts. Sift dry ingredients and stir in. Pour into greased loafpan and bake at 350° for 40 minutes. Yield: 1 loaf.

French Toast

2 eggs
6 tablespoons milk
⅛ teaspoon salt
6 slices bread
Hot shortening for frying

Beat eggs slightly. Stir in milk and salt. Dip the bread, one slice at a time, into the mixture. Melt shortening in heavy frying pan. When hot, place the bread slices in the pan. Turn to brown both sides. Yield: 3 to 6 servings.

Stickies

½ cup syrup
¼ cup butter or margarine
6 cold, sliced biscuits

Combine syrup and butter or margarine in a large skillet. Bring to a boil and boil until slightly thick. Turn heat down and add biscuits. Cook slowly, turning biscuits once. Serve hot. Yield: 6 servings.

Salt Rising Bread

Starter

1 cup milk
1 tablespoon sugar
7 tablespoons white cornmeal
1 teaspoon salt
2 cups lukewarm water
2 tablespoons sugar
3 tablespoons shortening
2 cups all-purpose flour

Scald 1 cup milk and stir in 1 tablespoon sugar, 7 tablespoons cornmeal, and 1 teaspoon salt. Place mixture in a jar, and cover with cheesecloth; set jar in water as hot as the hand can stand. Allow to stand for 6 to 7 hours in a warm place (115°) until it shows fermentation. The gas can be heard to escape when it has sufficiently fermented.

At the end of fermentation period, add 2 cups lukewarm water, 2 tablespoons sugar, 3 tablespoons shortening, and 2 cups all-purpose flour to make a sponge. Beat well; put in a container and set in a water bath canner; maintain heat at 115° until sponge is very light and full of bubbles.

To Make Bread

To this light sponge add about 8½ cups all-purpose flour, or enough to give a stiff dough. Knead for 10 minutes. Mold into about 4 loaves and place in greased loafpans. Cover and let rise to 2½ times the original bulk. Bake at 375° for 10 minutes, lower temperature to 350° and bake 25 minutes longer, or until loaves test done. Yield: about 4 loaves.

Old Virginia Sally Lunn

½ cup scalded milk
6 tablespoons shortening
1 package dry yeast
¼ cup very warm water
2 cups all-purpose flour
2 tablespoons sugar
½ teaspoon salt
2 eggs

Combine milk and shortening; cool until lukewarm. Meanwhile, dissolve yeast in very warm water. Combine flour, sugar, and salt in a large bowl; make a well in the center. Stir in yeast, then milk mixture. Let rise in a warm place for about 20 minutes. Stir in beaten eggs, and mix well. Cover with a clean towel and let rise until double in bulk (about 2 hours). Then beat well and turn into greased tubepan. Cover with a clean towel and let rise in warm place until doubled in bulk. Bake in two greased loafpans or a 10-inch tubepan at 425° for 15 to 20 minutes, or until done. Split across and butter, then cut into wedges. Serve hot. Or next day, toast wedges. Yield: 1 large Sally Lunn or 2 loaves.

Sweet Dough

½ cup milk
½ cup sugar
1½ teaspoons salt
¼ cup shortening
2 packages dry yeast
½ cup very warm water
2 eggs, beaten
5 cups all-purpose flour

Scald milk and stir in sugar, salt, and shortening. Cool to lukewarm. Dissolve yeast in very warm water. Stir until dissolved, then stir into the lukewarm milk mixture. Add beaten eggs and 3 cups flour. Beat until smooth, and stir in an additional 2 cups flour. Turn dough out onto lightly floured board and knead until smooth and elastic. Place in a greased bowl and brush top with soft shortening. Cover and let rise in a warm place, free from draft, until double in bulk (about 1 hour). Punch down and turn out onto lightly floured board. Use as desired to make any of the following sweet breads.

Kolaches

1 recipe Sweet Dough
  Filling (Choose one from list below.)

Prepare any of the fillings below. After dough rises, shape the Kolaches into ovals, or fold dough ½ inch thick and cut with a 2-inch biscuit cutter. Place about 1½ inches apart on greased baking sheet. Cover and let rise for 20 to 30 minutes. Make a depression in center of each and fill with 2 or 3 teaspoons filling. Pinch edges together tightly. Let rise for about 10 minutes, then bake at 400° for about 15 minutes. Yield: about 2 dozen.

Variations

Poppy Seed-Fruit Filling — Mix ½ cup cooked mashed apricots or prunes, ½ teaspoon cinnamon, ¼ cup sugar, and 2 tablespoons poppy seed.

Prune-Nut Filling — Mix together 1 cup cooked, mashed prunes, ¼ cup sugar, and ¼ cup chopped nuts.

Jam or Jelly Filling — Use any flavored jam or jelly; add spices or chopped nuts if desired.

Date-Nut Filling — Cook one 8-ounce package dates in small amount of water, mash, add sugar as desired, and beat until smooth. Nuts may be added if desired.

Cinnamon Buns

1 recipe Sweet Dough
1½ cups sugar
2 teaspoons ground cinnamon
⅔ cup raisins

Divide Sweet Dough in half. Roll out each half into an oblong 14 x 9 inches. Brush lightly with melted butter or margarine. Sprinkle each oblong with a mixture of sugar, cinnamon, and raisins. Roll up as for jellyroll to make roll 9 inches long. Seal edges firmly.

Cut into nine equal pieces. Place cut side up about 1 inch apart in greased pan. Cover, and let rise until doubled in bulk. Bake at 350° for about 35 minutes. Yield: about 2 dozen.

Basic Yeast Rolls

1 package dry yeast
¼ cup very warm water
½ cup scalded milk
2 tablespoons sugar
¾ teaspoon salt
2 tablespoons melted butter or
  margarine
1 egg, slightly beaten
2½ cups all-purpose flour

Dissolve dry yeast in very warm water according to directions on the package. Add milk which has been cooled to lukewarm, sugar, and salt. Allow to stand for 5 minutes. Add butter or margarine and egg, and mix well. Stir in flour and beat with spoon until dough forms a ball and follows spoon around the bowl. Brush top of dough with melted butter or margarine and cover with waxed paper or towel. Set bowl in warm water until dough is light and spongy, about 20 to 25 minutes. Turn out onto floured cloth or board, knead ½ minute. Shape, let rise, and bake at 400° for 10 to 12 minutes.

All the various rolls can be shaped from the same dough. A basic yeast dough can yield a variety of well shaped rolls.

1. One of the simplest of the rolls to shape is the Cloverleaf Roll. For this roll, form dough into small balls. Dip each into melted butter or margarine and place three balls in each section of a greased muffin pan. A nice, golden brown, crusty roll is the result. Split the hot roll three ways and drop a pat of butter or margarine in the center — simply good eating!

2. The Crescent-Shaped Roll is simple but elegant. Roll a ball of dough into circular shape about ¼ inch thick. Cut into pie-shaped pieces. Brush with melted butter or margarine and roll up, beginning at the wide end. Curve into crescents on greased baking sheet. Feature these attractive hot rolls at one of your special dinners and hear your guests ask for more.

3. Bowknot Rolls are just as the name implies, and just as simple to make. Roll a portion of dough under hands to form a rope about ½ inch in thickness. Cut into pieces about 6 inches long. Tie in knots. Place on greased baking sheet. Longer pieces of dough may be tied in double knots or coiled into "snails."

4. Fan Tan Rolls are attractive in their simplicity. To make these, roll dough into a very thin rectangular sheet. Brush with melted butter or margarine. Cut into strips about 1 inch wide. Stack six or seven strips on top of each other. Cut stacked strips into 1½-inch long pieces and place on end in greased muffin pans.

5. Parker House Rolls are easily made and are always favorites. Roll out dough and cut into rounds. Crease with dull edge of knife to one side of center. Brush lightly with melted butter or margarine. Fold larger side over smaller so edges meet. Seal. Put on greased baking sheet 1 inch apart.

Refrigerator Rolls

    1 package dry yeast
    ½ cup very warm water
    ½ cup shortening
    ½ cup sugar
    1 egg, beaten
    2 cups warm water
 1½ teaspoons salt
    About 8 cups all-purpose flour

Dissolve yeast in ½ cup very warm water. Cream shortening and sugar. Add beaten egg, water, salt, and softened yeast. Add flour, and mix well. Put in large greased bowl and grease the top. Cover and put in refrigerator.

When ready to use, shape the rolls and put in a greased pan. Let rise for about 3 hours and bake at 400° for 12 to 15 minutes. Yield: 4 to 5 dozen rolls.

Angel Food Cake

1½ cups cake flour
  2 teaspoons cream of tartar
2¼ cups sugar
 12 large egg whites
  ¼ teaspoon salt
  1 tablespoon freshly squeezed
     lemon juice
  1 teaspoon vanilla extract

Sift flour and measure. Add 1 teaspoon
cream of tartar, and sift five times.
Sift sugar and measure. Set aside. Beat
egg whites until they hold up in peaks.
Add salt and 1 teaspoon cream of
tartar. Add sugar, 2 tablespoonfuls at
a time. Add lemon juice and vanilla.
Fold in flour, 2 tablespoonfuls at a
time. Bake in a tubepan at 375° for 30
minutes and then reduce temperature
to 325° and bake for 30 minutes longer.

German's Sweet Chocolate Cake

  1 cup shortening
  2 cups sugar
  4 egg yolks, unbeaten
  1 teaspoon vanilla extract
  1 (¼-pound) package German's
     Sweet Chocolate
  ½ cup boiling water
2½ cups cake flour
  ½ teaspoon salt
  1 teaspoon soda
  1 cup buttermilk
  4 egg whites, stiffly beaten

Cream shortening; add sugar, then egg
yolks, one at a time. Add vanilla and
chocolate which has been melted in
boiling water, then cooled. Mix well.
Combine dry ingredients and add
alternately with buttermilk to creamed
mixture. Beat egg whites until stiff
and fold into batter. Pour into three
8- or 9-inch layer pans which have been
lined on bottom with waxed paper. Bake
at 350° for 35 to 40 minutes. Cool. Frost
with Coconut-Pecan Frosting.

Coconut-Pecan Frosting

  3 egg yolks
  1 cup evaporated milk
  1 cup sugar
  1 tablespoon butter or margarine
1½ cups flaked coconut
  1 cup chopped pecans
  1 teaspoon vanilla extract

Beat eggs and add milk, sugar, and
butter or margarine. Cook over medium
heat for about 12 minutes, stirring
constantly, until mixture thickens.
Remove from heat and add coconut,
pecans, and vanilla. Beat until cool and
of spreading consistency. Yield: enough
to cover tops of 3 (8- or 9-inch) layers.

White Cake

  1 cup shortening
  2 cups sugar
  3 cups all-purpose flour
  ½ teaspoon salt
  3 teaspoons baking powder
  1 cup milk
1½ teaspoons flavoring
  6 egg whites

Cream shortening. Add sugar gradually,
creaming until very light and fluffy. Sift
flour, salt, and baking powder together.
Add flour and milk alternately to
creamed mixture. Add flavoring. Fold in
stiffly beaten egg whites, and mix to a
smooth batter. Pour into greased, paper-
lined layer cakepans. Bake at 350° for
35 minutes.

Light Fruitcake

  2 cups all-purpose flour
  2 teaspoons baking powder
  ½ teaspoon salt
  1 pound coarsely chopped
     candied pineapple
  1 pound candied cherries, whole
1½ pounds coarsely chopped pitted dates
  4 eggs
  1 cup sugar
  2 pounds pecan halves (8 cups)

Combine flour, baking powder, and salt. Add fruits and mix well to coat with flour. Beat eggs until light and fluffy. Gradually beat in sugar. Add fruit-flour mixture and nuts; mix well with hands. Grease pans (two 9-inch springform pans or angel food pan and assorted molds as desired). Line pans with greased brown paper. Divide mixture between pans and press firmly into pans. Bake at 275° about 1 hour and 15 minutes or until cakes test done. Let cakes stand in pans about 10 minutes; turn out on racks and remove brown paper. Cool well before wrapping for storage. Yield: about 6 pounds.

Applesauce Cake

⅔ cup butter
2 cups sugar
4 egg yolks
¾ cup unsweetened applesauce
2½ cups all-purpose flour
3 teaspoons baking powder
1 teaspoon ground cloves
1 teaspoon ground cinnamon
½ teaspoon ground nutmeg
½ teaspoon ground allspice
2 tablespoons cocoa
½ cup milk
2 teaspoons vanilla extract
⅔ cup raisins
4 egg whites

Cream butter; add sugar and beat until well blended. Add beaten yolks and applesauce and beat until mixture is smooth. Sift flour with baking powder and spices five times. Add to creamed

mixture alternately with milk. When well mixed add vanilla, nuts, raisins, and fold in stiffly beaten egg whites. Turn into two 9-inch greased layer cakepans and bake at 350° for about 40 minutes. Put together with a caramel frosting.

Prune Cake

½ cup butter or margarine
1½ cups sugar
3 eggs
2¼ cups sifted cake flour
¾ teaspoon salt
1 teaspoon baking powder
2 teaspoons ground cinnamon
1 teaspoon ground nutmeg
¾ teaspoon ground cloves
¾ teaspoon ground allspice
1 teaspoon soda
1 cup buttermilk
1¼ cups chopped, cooked prunes

Cream butter or margarine and sugar until well blended. Add eggs one at a time and beat well. Sift dry ingredients and add alternately with the buttermilk. Fold in prunes. Bake in two (8-inch) layer cakepans at 350° for 35 to 40 minutes. Frost as desired. Yield: 2 (8-inch) layers.

Lane Cake

8 egg whites
1 cup butter or margarine
2 cups sugar
3½ cups all-purpose flour
3 teaspoons baking powder
1 cup milk
1 teaspoon vanilla extract (optional)

Beat egg whites until they hold a peak, but are not dry. Set aside, then cream butter or margarine and sugar well. Sift flour and baking powder together and add to creamed mixture alternately with milk. Fold in beaten egg whites and vanilla. Bake in four layers at 350° until brown.

Filling

      1 cup chopped nuts
      1 cup flaked coconut
      1 cup seedless raisins
    ½ cup butter or margarine
      2 cups sugar
      8 egg yolks
    ¾ cup grape juice

Grind nuts, coconut, and raisins. Put these in a saucepan with the butter or margarine, sugar, and egg yolks. Cook for 15 to 20 minutes. Stir in grape juice to thin filling. Spread between layers, and use a white frosting for top and sides of cake.

Southern Coconut Cake

      4 cups sifted cake flour
      5 teaspoons baking powder
    1½ teaspoons salt
      6 egg whites
    ½ cup sugar
      1 cup all-vegetable shortening
      2 cups sugar
      2 cups milk
      1 teaspoon vanilla extract
      1 teaspoon almond extract
         Zesty Lemon Filling
         Coconut-Marshmallow Frosting
         Flaked coconut

Combine flour, baking powder, and salt. Beat egg whites until foamy and gradually add ½ cup sugar; set aside. Continue beating until meringue will hold up in stiff peaks. Cream shortening and gradually add the 2 cups sugar; cream until light and fluffy. Add flour mixture alternately with milk, a small amount at a time, beating well after each addition. Add vanilla and almond extracts. Add beaten egg whites and fold thoroughly into batter.

Line bottom of three 9-inch cakepans with waxed paper. Lightly grease and flour pans. Pour in batter. Bake at 375° for 20 to 25 minutes, or until cake tests done. Spread Zesty Lemon Filling between the layers and ice cake with Coconut-Marshmallow Frosting. Sprinkle cake with flaked coconut.

Zesty Lemon Filling

      1 cup sugar
      3 tablespoons cornstarch
    ½ teaspoon salt
      1 cup boiling water
      2 tablespoons grated lemon rind
    ½ cup freshly squeezed lemon juice
      2 tablespoons butter or margarine

Combine all ingredients. Bring to a full rolling boil, stirring occasionally. Turn down the heat and boil for 1 minute, stirring all the time. Let cool at room temperature. Beat well before spreading on cake. Yield: enough filling for 2 (8- or 9-inch) layers.

Coconut-Marshmallow Frosting

      1 cup sugar
    ½ cup boiling water
    ¼ teaspoon vinegar
      2 egg whites, stiffly beaten
    10 marshmallows, quartered
      1 cup thin-flaked coconut

Place sugar, water, and vinegar in a saucepan and cook over low heat until sugar is dissolved. Cover, and cook for 2 minutes. Remove cover and cook until the soft-ball stage is reached (238° to 240°). Pour in a thin stream over stiffly beaten egg whites, beating constantly. Add marshmallows, and continue stirring until cool and thick enough to spread. Spread on cake and sprinkle with the coconut. Yield: enough frosting for 2 (8-inch) layers.

Devil's Food Cake

1 cup butter or vegetable shortening
2 cups sugar
4 eggs
2 cups all-purpose flour
¾ cup cocoa
1 teaspoon soda
1 cup strong cold coffee
1 teaspoon vanilla extract

Cream butter or shortening until soft
and creamy. Add sugar gradually, beating until light and fluffy. Add eggs and
beat thoroughly. Measure flour and cocoa
and sift together. Dissolve soda in 2
tablespoons coffee, and add to rest of the
coffee. Add dry ingredients alternately
with coffee. Beat until well blended. Add
vanilla. Pour into two 9-inch greased
layer pans. Bake at 350° for about
30 minutes. Yield: 2 (9-inch) layers.

Kentucky Jam Cake

½ cup butter
2 cups sugar
3 eggs
3 cups all-purpose flour
1 teaspoon soda
¼ teaspoon each ground cloves, cinnamon,
   and allspice, if desired
⅓ cup cocoa
½ cup buttermilk
   About ⅓ cup coffee
2 cups strawberry jam

Cream butter and sugar until light and
fluffy. Add eggs one at a time, beating
well after each addition. Combine dry
ingredients; add alternately to creamed
mixture with milk and coffee. Stir in
jam. Bake in three greased 8-inch layer
pans at 325° for 25 minutes or until cake
tests done. Do not overbake. Cool
and frost.

Apple Dapple Cake

3 eggs
1½ cups salad oil
2 cups sugar
3 cups all-purpose flour
1 teaspoon salt
1 teaspoon soda
2 teaspoons vanilla extract
3 cups chopped apples
1½ cups chopped pecans

Mix eggs, salad oil, and sugar, and
blend well. Add flour, salt, and soda
mixed well. Add vanilla, chopped apples,
and nuts. Put into greased 8- or 9-inch
tubepan. Bake at 350° for one hour.
While cake is still hot, pour hot Topping
over it in the pan.

Topping

1 cup brown sugar
¼ cup milk
1 stick margarine

Combine all ingredients and cook for
2½ minutes. Pour hot Topping over hot
cake in pan. Let set until cold; when
completely cold, remove cake with
Topping from pan.

Caramel Frosting

3 cups firmly packed brown sugar
1 cup water
1 tablespoon butter or margarine
1 teaspoon vanilla extract
   Cream or rich milk, to soften

Boil the sugar and water until the syrup
reaches the soft-ball stage (238° to
240°). Add the butter or margarine and
vanilla and remove from heat. Let cool,
then beat until thick and creamy. Add
cream until consistency to spread. Yield:
enough frosting for 2 (9-inch) layers.

Divinity

2 cups sugar
½ cup white corn syrup
½ cup boiling water
2 egg whites, beaten
1 teaspoon vanilla extract
Cherries (optional)
Nuts (optional)

Combine sugar, corn syrup, and water.
Cook over moderate heat until mixture
spins a thread when dropped from a
spoon. Gradually add to the beaten egg
whites, beating all the while. Add vanilla
and beat until candy loses its gloss and
stands in peaks. Drop by teaspoonfuls
onto waxed paper. Top with cherries or
nuts, if desired. Yield: 1½ pounds.

Million-Dollar Fudge

4¼ cups sugar
6 tablespoons butter or margarine
1 (14½-ounce) can evaporated milk
2 (6-ounce) packages chocolate pieces
1 (8-ounce) jar marshmallow cream
4 cups chopped nuts

Boil together the sugar, butter or margarine, and evaporated milk for about 7
minutes after first bubbles appear, or
until the soft-ball stage is reached. Put
chocolate pieces, marshmallow cream,
and nuts into a large bowl. Pour syrup
over and stir until chocolate is dissolved.
Beat until cool and creamy. Drop on
waxed paper or pour into greased pan,
cool, and cut into serving pieces. Yield:
about 2 pounds.

Oldtime Pralines

3 cups sugar
1 cup cream or rich milk
1 teaspoon grated orange rind
1 cup sugar
1 teaspoon vanilla extract
*2 cups pecans or mixed nuts (pecans and
  black walnuts)*
Dash salt

Boil the 3 cups sugar with the cream and
rind in a large, deep kettle, until it forms
a soft ball (as for fudge) when dropped
in cold water. While this syrup is cooking, melt the remaining cup of sugar in
a heavy frying pan, stirring constantly
until it reaches the pale golden brown
caramel stage. When both syrups are
ready, carefully add the caramelized
sugar to the first syrup, stirring with a
long spoon, and being careful not to get
burned when it foams up. Test immediately for the soft-ball stage; if un-
satisfactory, remove from heat and let
cool almost to lukewarm. Then add the
vanilla, nuts, and salt, and beat until
stiff and creamy, as for fudge. Drop in
fat cakes onto a buttered cookie sheet.

Allow to cool before removing from
sheet. Yield: 3 dozen.

Pulled Mints

2 cups sugar
1 cup water
¼ cup butter or margarine
Few drops oil of peppermint
Food coloring

Combine sugar and water. Cook slowly,
stirring constantly until mixture boils.
Add butter or margarine. Boil slowly
without stirring to the hard-ball stage
(258° to 261° on your candy thermometer). To test candy, if you do not have
a thermometer, pour from a spoon into
cup of cool water, circling spoon to form
a coil. This coil should be brittle. Re
move immediately from heat and pour
out in a circle on a cold marble slab. Try
to make thickness of circle the same
around. When candy is brittle on surface
and soft in center, loosen from slab. Fold
candy and pull gently but firmly with
tips of fingers. Smear a few drops of
food coloring and oil of peppermint in
center of candy. Continue folding and

pulling until color is distributed. Stretch into a long rope, continually turning, and cut off pieces into desired lengths with scissors. Place pieces on cloth to dry overnight. When hard and dry, put into airtight container and mints will become creamy. Yield: about 3 dozen.

Yam Pralines

    3 cups sugar
    1 cup light cream
 1¼ cups cooked, mashed sweet potatoes
       Dash salt
    1 cup firmly packed brown sugar
    2 cups chopped pecans

Combine sugar, cream, sweet potatoes, and salt in a heavy saucepan. Mix well. Cook over medium heat until mixture reaches soft-ball stage (234°). Stir occasionally. Melt brown sugar in a heavy skillet over medium heat. Then quickly add melted sugar and pecans to candy mixture. Blend thoroughly. Remove from heat and drop by spoonfuls onto greased cookie sheet. Allow pralines to cool until crystallized. Yield: about 2 dozen.

Date Roll

    3 cups sugar
 1½ cups milk
    2 cups chopped dates
    1 cup pecans
    1 teaspoon vanilla extract
    1 tablespoon butter

Boil sugar and milk until it forms a soft ball in water (236°). Do not scrape sides of pan. Add dates and nuts and cook until it forms a firm ball in water (240°). Add vanilla, and remove from heat. Let stand until lukewarm. Beat as fudge. When it begins to thicken, pour onto damp cloth and roll. Let stand for 24 hours; then slice. Date Roll can be kept in a damp cloth in a cool place for several weeks. Yield: about 1 pound.

Candied Grapefruit Peel

    1 large grapefruit
 1½ cups sugar
       Coloring (optional)

Cover grapefruit peel (cut into strips) with water and bring to a brisk boil. Drain well, and repeat five times to remove bitter flavor. After last draining, cover with sugar and do not add water. Stir over low heat until syrup forms. Add coloring, if desired. Cook until peel absorbs all the syrup. Remove to platter covered with granulated sugar and let peel take up as much sugar as it will hold. Store in airtight containers. Yield: 3 dozen.

Peanut Brittle

    2 cups sugar
    1 cup white corn syrup
  ½ cup water
    1 teaspoon salt
    2 tablespoons butter
    2 cups raw peanuts
    2 teaspoons vanilla extract
 1½ teaspoons soda

Mix first four ingredients and bring to boil. Cover and boil for 3 minutes. Remove cover and boil to 250°, or to a hard-ball stage, then add butter and peanuts. Cook slowly to 300° or a hard-crack stage, then stir vanilla and soda into mixture quickly. Pour onto greased slab or platter. Let stand for 1 minute or so, then turn over like a pancake, and pull from edges to desired thinness. Yield: 2 pounds.

Note: Roasted peanuts may be used and added at the last. Never pour onto tin or enamelware.

Mexican Pecan Candy

2 *cups sugar*
1 *cup milk*
2 *tablespoons butter*
2 *tablespoons white corn syrup*
½ *teaspoon salt*
½ *teaspoon soda*
1 *cup chopped pecans*
1 *teaspoon vanilla extract*

Mix all ingredients except pecans and
vanilla in a large saucepan, and bring to
a boil. When mixture comes to a boil, add
pecans and cook until it reaches 234°, or
until it forms a soft ball when dropped
into cold water. Add vanilla and beat
until creamy. Drop by spoonfuls onto
waxed paper, or spread in buttered pan
and cut into squares. Yield: about 2
dozen.

Fruited Molasses Taffy

1¼ *cups molasses*
1 *cup sugar*
1 *tablespoon butter or margarine*
⅔ *cup ground dates or raisins*
½ *cup chopped nuts or coconut*
1 *tablespoon molasses*

Cook first three ingredients together in
saucepan until syrup separates into
threads which are hard, but not brittle
(270° or soft-crack stage). Stir constantly. Pour at once onto greased platter
or cookie sheet. As edges cool, fold them
toward center with spatula or they will
harden before center is ready to pull.
(Do not disturb that part of taffy which
has not cooled, or candy will stick to
pan.) When taffy is cool enough to pull,
fold into a ball. Butter fingers lightly,
and pull until candy is light in color.
Flatten to a 5- x 12- x ¼-inch rectangle,
using palms of hands or lightly greased
rolling pin. Mix last three ingredients
together, and with buttered fingers
spread it thinly to ½ inch from edge,
over surface of candy. Roll as for jellyroll, starting from the side rather than
from end. Stretch roll into a long rope
½ inch wide. Cut into 1-inch pieces.
Wrap each piece in waxed paper. Yield:
about 3 dozen.

Penuche

1 *(1-pound) box brown sugar*
¾ *cup light cream or half-and-half*
1 *tablespoon white corn syrup*
2 *tablespoons butter*
1 *teaspoon vanilla extract*
1 *cup coarsely chopped walnuts or pecans*

Measure all ingredients except vanilla
and nuts into large saucepan. Heat to
boiling, stirring constantly, and boil
gently to 238° or until a few drops form
a soft ball in cold water. (Don't worry
if mixture curdles; beating will make it
smooth.) Remove from heat and let
stand without stirring until bottom of
pan feels lukewarm. Stir in vanilla and
nuts; then beat with spoon until thick
and creamy and mixture begins to lose
its gloss. Pour into buttered 8-inch
square pan. Cut into squares while warm.
Yield: about 1 pound.

To Make Good Candy

Candies are energy foods; with fruits
and nuts added they offer additional
nutrients. Candies are welcome gifts at
any season of the year, and the boxes of
homemade candy are always the first to
be sold at bazaars.

Candymaking, to be successful, is more
than a matter of luck. Just as in any
other cooking process, there are some
special rules. With careful attention to
the rules that apply, there is no reason
why you cannot make perfect candy
every time. Here are some of the rules
to follow:

Organize Your Work: Check to see that you have all the equipment and ingredients needed before starting candy.

Right Equipment: A large, heavy saucepan is best for candymaking. Select one that will allow the mixture to boil up without boiling over. Wooden spoons are preferable to metal ones since they are more comfortable to hold and will not scratch the pan. Remove the spoon while the candy is cooking.

Thermometer: A candy thermometer is very helpful because it is important to cook candy at exactly the right temperature and to the right stage. Some people can judge fairly well by dropping a small bit of the candy into cold water, but this is not entirely dependable and takes a great deal of experience.

Stirring: Occasional stirring of candies made with milk or cream is often necessary to keep the candy from sticking or scorching. If fruit or nuts are cooked in the candy, it is usually necessary to stir it.

Using Lid: A tight-fitting lid on the saucepan is necessary for the first few minutes of cooking. As soon as the syrup has begun to boil, the lid should be removed and the cooking completed. The steam that forms in the first few minutes helps to dissolve the sugar crystals which might form on the sides of the pan.

Heat Control: Candy in which milk or cream is used should be cooked at medium temperature to prevent scorching. Candy using water or fruit juice may be cooked at a higher temperature.

Weather: A clear day is better for making candy, since there is less moisture in the air. If candy is made on a cloudy or damp day, it should be cooked to a slightly firmer stage.

Beating Candy: Candy to be beaten should always be allowed to cool first. For a fine grained, creamy product, allow the candy to cool to 110° before beating.

Ingredients: All ingredients used in candies should be fresh and of good quality. When measuring brown sugar, remember to pack it firmly into the measuring cup. In recipes calling for coconut, you may use fresh coconut grated, or canned, packaged, or frozen. There are several types of coconut on the market . . . flaked, shredded, and grated. Any of these may be used. However, the flaked makes a smoother product for dropping or for cutting into squares.

Testing the Candy

In using a candy thermometer, the following degrees will show the degree of doneness of the candy.

Soft-ball stage	234° to 240°
Firm-ball stage	244° to 250°
Hard-ball stage	250° to 265°
Hard-crack stage	290° to 310°

If you have no candy thermometer, you may use the cold water test, although it is not as accurate. In making these tests, use fresh, cold water each time you test a sample. Drop a very little of the boiling syrup into a cup of cold water. Be sure to remove the syrup from the heat while testing is being done. When the syrup in the cold water can be gathered up between the fingers into a ball that holds its shape fairly well, it has reached the soft-ball stage.

The firm-ball stage has been reached when the ball will hold its shape.

When the ball reaches the stage that it holds its shape and is hard enough to be rolled on an oiled surface, the hard-ball stage has been reached.

The hard-crack stage is reached when the ball removed from the water is quite firm and cracks when knocked against the side of the cup.

Peanut Butter Cookies

¼ cup vegetable shortening
¼ cup butter or margarine
½ cup white sugar
½ cup firmly packed brown sugar
1 egg
½ cup peanut butter
¼ teaspoon vanilla extract
1½ cups all-purpose flour
1 teaspoon soda
¼ teaspoon salt

Cream shortening and butter or margarine together until light and fluffy. Add sugars, and cream until smooth. Add the egg, and beat well. Beat in peanut butter and vanilla. Combine flour, soda, and salt and add to creamed mixture. Roll dough into balls about 1 inch in diameter. Place on greased cookie sheets and flatten by pressing with tip of teaspoon. Bake at 400° for 10 to 12 minutes. Yield: 4 dozen.

Festive Fruit Cookies

½ cup shortening
½ cup firmly packed brown sugar
¾ cup white sugar
1 teaspoon vanilla extract
1 egg, slightly beaten
1 (6-ounce) can frozen orange juice concentrate
2½ cups all-purpose flour
1 teaspoon soda
½ teaspoon baking powder
¼ teaspoon salt
¾ cup flaked coconut
¾ cup chopped nuts
2 cups powdered sugar
½ cup soft butter

Cream shortening and sugars until light and fluffy. Add vanilla and egg. Add ½ cup orange juice, reserving remainder for frosting. Stir until well blended. Combine flour, soda, baking powder, and salt. Add to orange mixture, stirring until smooth. Add coconut and nuts.

Drop by teaspoonfuls onto ungreased baking sheets. Bake at 350° for 9 to 11 minutes. Remove to cooling rack. Blend sugar with butter and reserved orange concentrate. Frost hot cookies. Yield: 5 dozen.

Sand Tarts

2 cups all-purpose flour
1½ teaspoons baking powder
½ cup butter or margarine
1 cup sugar
1 egg
Egg white
Sugar
Cinnamon

Sift flour with baking powder. Cream butter or margarine thoroughly; add sugar, and cream until light and fluffy. Add egg and flour. Blend and chill until firm enough to roll ⅛ inch thick. Cut with doughnut cutter. Brush with egg white and sprinkle with mixture of sugar and cinnamon. Bake on ungreased cookie sheets at 375° for 10 minutes. Yield: 4 dozen.

Black Walnut Cookies

2⅓ cups all-purpose flour
2 teaspoons baking powder
1 teaspoon salt
1 cup shortening
¾ cup white or brown sugar
½ cup light or dark corn syrup
2 eggs
1 teaspoon vanilla extract
1 cup coarsely chopped black walnuts
¼ cup milk

Combine flour, baking powder, and salt. Cream shortening. Add sugar gradually and cream until light and fluffy. Add corn syrup and blend thoroughly. Add eggs, one at a time, beating well after each addition. Stir in vanilla and walnuts. Add dry ingredients alternately with milk. Drop by teaspoonfuls onto greased baking sheet. Bake at 375° for 12 to 15 minutes. Yield: 5 dozen.

Note: Walnuts or pecans may be substituted for the black walnuts.

Gingersnaps

1 cup molasses
½ cup shortening
¼ teaspoon salt
3 cups all-purpose flour
1 teaspoon soda
2 teaspoons ground ginger

Heat molasses and shortening. Mix and sift dry ingredients and add to first mixture (need not wait for it to cool). Thoroughly chill, toss on lightly floured board, roll very thin, and cut. Handle quickly and do not let get warm. Bake on greased cookie sheets at 375° for 8 to 10 minutes. Yield: 4 dozen.

Butter-Pecan Cookies

1 cup butter or margarine
¾ cup firmly packed brown sugar
¾ cup white sugar
2 eggs
1 teaspoon vanilla extract
2¼ cups all-purpose flour
1 teaspoon soda
½ teaspoon salt
1 cup chopped pecans

Stir in peanut butter. Combine dry ingredients; stir into creamed mixture. Drop by teaspoonfuls onto ungreased cookie sheets. Press with back of floured fork to make a criss-cross design. Bake at 350° for about 10 minutes, or until lightly browned. Yield: about 6 dozen.

Coconut-Gumdrop Cookies

1 cup shortening
1 cup firmly packed dark brown sugar
1 cup white sugar
2 eggs, well beaten
1 teaspoon vanilla extract
2 cups all-purpose flour
¼ teaspoon salt
1 teaspoon soda
1 teaspoon baking powder
1 cup flaked coconut
2 cups uncooked oatmeal
1 cup pecans, chopped
1 cup gumdrops, chopped

Cream shortening and sugar; add well beaten eggs and vanilla and mix well. Sift dry ingredients together and add to Cream butter or shortening. Add sugar and cream together. Stir in vanilla. Add eggs, one at a time, beating well. Sift flour and soda; add to creamed mixture, stirring until blended. Stir in oatmeal and peanuts. Drop batter by teaspoonfuls onto well greased cookie sheet. Bake at 400° for 10 to 15 minutes, or until lightly browned. Yield: 5 dozen.

Refrigerator Cookies

1 cup shortening
½ cup brown sugar
½ cup white sugar
1 egg, beaten
2 tablespoons orange juice
2 tablespoons grated orange rind
2 cups all-purpose flour
¼ teaspoon soda
½ cup pecans, chopped fine

Cream shortening and sugar. Add the beaten egg, orange juice, and grated rind, beating until smooth. Sift flour and soda together, and add to creamed mixture. Stir in chopped pecans. Shape into a roll and chill overnight in refrigerator. Slice thin and bake on ungreased cookie sheets at 375° for 10 to 12 minutes. Yield: 5 dozen.

Sumrall Cookies

1 (1-pound) box brown sugar
4 eggs
2 cups all-purpose flour
1 teaspoon baking powder
½ teaspoon soda
2 cups pecans
1 teaspoon vanilla extract

Combine brown sugar and eggs and beat well. Add flour which has been combined with baking powder and soda. Stir in pecans and vanilla. Mix well with hands. Spread batter on a greased 15- x 10- x 1-inch cookie sheet. Bake at 350° for about 25 minutes. Cut into bars while hot. Yield: about 4 dozen.

Crisp Almond Cookies

1 cup butter
1 cup sugar
1 cup thick sour cream
⅛ teaspoon soda
2 egg yolks
1½ teaspoons grated lemon rind
1 teaspoon soda
½ teaspoon salt
3 to 3⅓ cups all-purpose flour
¾ cup almonds
2 tablespoons sugar

Combine butter, 1 cup sugar, cream, and ⅛ teaspoon soda in heavy saucepan. Place over heat. Stir until sugar is dissolved. Boil, stirring occasionally, until thick (10 to 15 minutes). Cool to lukewarm. Beat in egg yolks, lemon rind, 1 teaspoon soda, and salt. Add enough flour to make a medium-stiff dough. Roll dough, ½ teaspoon at a time, in palm of hands to form small balls. Place 3 inches apart on ungreased cookie sheet. Press flat with bottom of glass dipped in sugar. Sprinkle with mixture of almonds and 2 tablespoons sugar. Bake on ungreased cookie sheets 325° for 10 to 12 minutes or until edges are browned. Yield: 10 dozen.

Williamsburg Cookies

1 egg white
¼ teaspoon salt
1 cup firmly packed brown sugar
1 cup chopped nuts
1 tablespoon all-purpose flour
½ teaspoon vanilla extract

Beat egg white until stiff; add salt. Add brown sugar gradually. Chop nuts and sprinkle with flour, then add to egg white mixture. Add vanilla and drop by teaspoonfuls onto greased cookie sheet. Bake at 275° for 15 minutes. Allow cookies to cool for 1 minute before removing from cookie sheet. Yield: 2 dozen.

Orange Cookies

⅔ cup butter or margarine
1¼ cups sugar
2 eggs
3 cups all-purpose flour
1½ teaspoons salt
2 teaspoons baking powder
Juice of 1 orange
Grated rind of 1½ oranges

Cream butter or margarine and sugar. Beat in eggs. Sift flour, measure, then sift together with other dry ingredients. Add to creamed mixture. Then add orange juice and grated orange rind. Mix well. Chill. Roll thin, cut, bake on ungreased cookie sheets at 400° for about 8 minutes. Yield: 4 dozen.

Confederate Jumbles

¾ cup butter
1½ cups sugar
3 eggs
1 teaspoon baking powder
¼ teaspoon salt
About 2 cups all-purpose flour
3 tablespoons milk

Cream butter and sugar. Add eggs, and beat well. Sift baking powder, salt, and flour together and add to the creamed mixture. Add the milk. This dough should be stiff enough to roll. Roll and sprinkle with sugar. Cut and bake on a greased cookie sheet at 350° for 8 to 10 minutes. Yield: about 4 dozen.

Black Walnut Drop Cookies

½ cup shortening
⅓ cup butter or margarine
¼ cup powdered sugar
1 teaspoon vanilla extract
2 tablespoons thick cream
2 cups all-purpose flour
1 teaspoon soda
2 cups chopped black walnuts
   Sifted powdered sugar

Cream shortening and butter or margarine together. Add sugar, and cream until light. Stir in vanilla and thick cream. Sift flour and soda together. Add nuts, and chop the nuts in the flour mixture. Stir into creamed mixture. Shape into small balls the size of hickory nuts. Place on cookie sheet and bake at 325° until a delicate brown, about 20 to 30 minutes. When cool, roll in sifted powdered sugar. Yield: 4 dozen.

Old-Fashioned Sugar Cookies

1 cup shortening (part butter)
1½ cups sugar
2 eggs
2¾ cups all-purpose flour
2 teaspoons soda
2 teaspoons cream of tartar
½ teaspoon salt
2 tablespoons sugar
2 teaspoons ground cinnamon

Cream together shortening and 1½ cups sugar. Add eggs, and beat until light and fluffy. Combine flour, soda, cream of tartar, and salt and add to creamed mixture. Chill for at least 1 hour in refrigerator. Roll in a mixture of 2 tablespoons sugar and 2 teaspoons ground cinnamon. Cut into desired shapes. Bake on ungreased cookie sheets at 350° for about 10 to 12 minutes. Yield: 4 to 5 dozen.

Ladyfingers

3 egg whites
   Pinch salt
⅓ cup powdered sugar
2 egg yolks
¼ teaspoon vanilla extract
⅓ cup all-purpose flour

Beat egg whites until stiff; add salt. Fold in powdered sugar. Add beaten egg yolks. Add vanilla, then fold in flour. Form into finger shapes on slightly greased and floured pan. Bake at 350° for about 10 minutes. Yield: 2 dozen.

Oatmeal Lace Cookies

2 tablespoons melted shortening
1 cup sugar
2 eggs
½ teaspoon vanilla extract
½ teaspoon almond extract
¾ teaspoon salt
2¼ cups uncooked oatmeal
2 cups uncooked oatmeal

Combine shortening and sugar. Add eggs, and beat until light and fluffy. Add vanilla and almond extracts. Mix salt and baking powder with oatmeal and add to first mixture. Drop by teaspoonfuls onto greased cookie sheet, 2 inches apart. Bake for 12 to 15 minutes at 350°. Remove from cookie sheet *immediately* after baking. Yield: 3 dozen.

Fresh Peach Ice Cream

        6 cups light cream
        4 cups milk
    1 ½ cups sugar
        ¼ teaspoon salt
        2 teaspoons vanilla extract
        ½ teaspoon almond extract
        4 eggs
        4 cups peaches
    1 ½ cups sugar

Combine cream and milk. Stir in 1 ½ cups sugar, salt, flavoring, and beaten eggs. Add peaches which have been mashed and combined with 1 ½ cups sugar. Place in crank-type freezer, or refrigerator trays, and freeze. Yield: 1 gallon.

Chocolate Ice Cream

    1 ½ squares unsweetened chocolate
        or ¼ cup cocoa
        1 cup sugar
        ⅓ cup hot water
        Dash salt
        1 tablespoon vanilla extract
        1 quart thin cream

Melt chocolate. Combine melted chocolate (or cocoa), sugar, and water; cook until smooth and sugar is dissolved. Add salt and vanilla and cool. Add to cream and freeze. Yield: 8 servings.

Rich Vanilla Ice Cream

        6 cups milk
        8 teaspoons cornstarch
        2 cups sugar
        ½ teaspoon salt
        4 eggs
        2 cups milk
        1 quart cream
        2 tablespoons vanilla extract

Scald 6 cups milk over hot water. Mix cornstarch, sugar, and salt; add scalded milk, stirring until sugar is dissolved. Cook in top of double boiler over boiling water for 20 minutes, stirring constantly, until slightly thickened. Beat eggs, and beat in remaining 2 cups milk; gradually stir hot mixture into egg mixture. Return mixture to top of double boiler and cook over boiling water for 10 minutes, stirring constantly. Cool and add cream and vanilla extract. Chill. Pour into a chilled 1-gallon ice cream freezer can. Freeze. Yield: 1 gallon.

Buttermilk Sherbet

        2 cups buttermilk
        ⅔ cup sugar
        Pinch salt
        1 cup crushed pineapple and juice
        1 teaspoon vanilla extract
        1 egg white, beaten

Combine buttermilk, sugar, salt, pineapple, and vanilla. Pour into freezing tray and freeze to a soft consistency. Beat egg white until stiff. Transfer frozen mixture to a mixing bowl and beat until fluffy, then fold in egg white. Return to freezing tray and freeze. Yield: 3 cups.

Strawberry Ice Cream

    12 eggs, well beaten
        3 cups sugar
        1 tablespoon all-purpose flour
        ½ teaspoon salt
        3 teaspoons vanilla extract
        2 cups half-and-half (cream and milk)
        1 cup whipping cream
        4 to 6 cups fresh strawberries, crushed
        Whole milk

Beat eggs. Combine sugar, flour, and salt and gradually add to beaten eggs; mix well. Add vanilla extract, half-and-half, cream, and crushed strawberries. Mix well and put into bucket of 1 ½- or 2-gallon freezer. Add milk to within one-third of top of bucket. Freeze until firm. Yield: 1 ½ gallons.

Old-Fashioned Bread Pudding

2 cups scalded milk
¼ cup butter or margarine
2 eggs, slightly beaten
½ cup sugar
¼ teaspoon salt
1 teaspoon ground cinnamon
3 cups soft bread cubes (about 5 slices)
½ cup seedless raisins

Combine milk and butter or margarine. Stir milk mixture gradually into beaten eggs; add sugar, salt, and cinnamon. Put bread cubes and raisins in 1½-quart baking dish; pour milk mixture over; stir gently to moisten bread. Place in a pan of hot water. Bake at 350° for 40 to 45 minutes or until knife inserted 1 inch from edge comes out clean. Remove from hot water. Serve warm or cold. Yield: 6 servings.

Baked Custard

3 cups milk
6 tablespoons sugar
¼ teaspoon salt
3 eggs, slightly beaten
1 teaspoon vanilla extract
1 tablespoon butter or margarine
   Ground nutmeg or cinnamon

Scald milk with sugar and salt. Stir slowly into beaten eggs, and add vanilla. Strain into custard cups or large baking dish, dot with butter or margarine, and add a dash or two of nutmeg or cinnamon. Set cups or baking dish in a shallow pan of hot water to come almost to top. Set on center rack of oven and bake at 325° until done, about 30 minutes. To test for doneness, insert knife in center of custard. When knife comes out clean, custard is done. Be careful not to overbake, as baking too long or at too high temperature will result in wheying or "weeping" of the cooled custard. Serve directly from custard cups, or spoon out into individual serving dishes and serve with any desired dessert sauce on top: chocolate, ground peppermint candy, or melted marshmallows. Yield: 6 servings.

Rice Pudding

2 eggs
2 cups milk
1¼ cups cold, cooked rice
1 cup seedless raisins
½ cup sugar
¼ teaspoon salt
1 teaspoon vanilla extract
   Dash ground cinnamon and nutmeg

Beat eggs until light and thick, and add to the milk. Lightly mix in the other ingredients. Place in a buttered 1½-quart casserole. Bake in a shallow pan of water at 350° for 1 hour, or until mixture is firm. Yield: 6 servings.

Banana Pudding

¾ cup sugar, divided
⅓ cup all-purpose flour
¼ teaspoon salt
2 cups scalded milk
2 eggs, separated
1 teaspoon vanilla extract
25 vanilla wafers
4 bananas, sliced

Blend ½ cup sugar, flour, and salt in top of double boiler. Add milk and cook until thick, stirring constantly. Cover and cook for 15 minutes. Beat egg yolks, combine with custard, and cook 2 minutes longer. Add vanilla. Line flat baking dish with vanilla wafers. Add sliced bananas. Top with custard. Repeat layers, if necessary. Beat egg whites until stiff, add remaining ¼ cup sugar and spread over custard. Bake at 350° about 12 to 15 minutes. Yield: 6 servings.

Plum Pudding

1	cup seedless raisins
1½	cups mixed diced candied fruits
½	cup chopped walnuts
1	cup all-purpose flour
2	eggs, beaten
¾	cup molasses
¾	cup buttermilk
½	cup finely chopped suet
¼	cup cold, strong coffee
1	cup fine, dry breadcrumbs
¾	teaspoon soda
¼	teaspoon ground cloves
¼	teaspoon ground allspice
¼	teaspoon ground cinnamon
¼	teaspoon ground nutmeg
¾	teaspoon salt

Combine fruits, walnuts, and ½ cup flour. Mix together eggs, molasses, buttermilk, suet, and coffee. Combine remaining flour, crumbs, soda, spices, salt, and add to egg mixture. Add to fruit, and mix well. Pour into well greased 1½-quart mold. Set on rack in deep pan; add boiling water to about 1 inch below cover of mold. Cover. Steam for 1½ to 2 hours. Yield: 10 to 12 servings.

Glazed Baked Apples

1½	cups sugar
½	teaspoon ground cinnamon
1½	cups water
1	tablespoon freshly squeezed lemon juice
2	tablespoons freshly squeezed orange juice
6	to 8 baking apples
¼	teaspoon red vegetable coloring

Combine 1 cup of the sugar with cinnamon in saucepan. Add water and strained fruit juices. Bring to a boil, and boil for 5 minutes. Wash medium-sized apples and remove about three-fourths of the core of each apple, cutting from stem end and leaving a solid base. Peel, leaving about ¼ inch of peel at base. Place in a shallow baking pan and pour boiling syrup over apples. Bake at 375° for about 30 minutes or until apples are tender. Baste frequently. Remove from oven when done.

To remaining ½ cup sugar, add the red vegetable coloring and stir with a fork until all sugar is thoroughly colored. Sprinkle tops of each apple with a little of the colored sugar. Put under broiler about 4 inches from heat. Baste with syrup in pan and continue sprinkling on more sugar until apples are glazed, about 15 minutes.

Remove from broiler and place apples on serving platter. If syrup is still somewhat thin, cook down until quite thick. Pour over apples, filling centers well. Cool until syrup is set, or chill in refrigerator if to be used for a meat accompaniment. Yield: 6 to 8 servings.

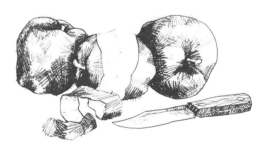

Southern Sweet Potato Pudding

2	cups grated raw sweet potatoes
¼	cup melted butter or margarine
1	teaspoon grated lemon peel
¼	teaspoon ground ginger
½	teaspoon ground cinnamon
¼	teaspoon ground cloves
1	cup brown sugar, firmly packed
2	eggs, well beaten
½	cup chopped nuts
	Whipped cream (optional)

Grate peeled potatoes with fine grater. Measure and combine with next six ingredients. Add to well beaten eggs and blend. Pour into greased 1-quart casserole. Top with nuts. Bake at 325° for 1 hour. Serve warm — plain or with whipped cream. Yield: 6 to 8 servings.

Indian Pudding

4   cups milk
½   cup plain cornmeal
2   tablespoons butter or margarine
½   cup molasses
1   teaspoon salt
1   teaspoon ground cinnamon
¼   teaspoon ground ginger
2   eggs

Scald the milk. Put cornmeal in top of double boiler, and pour in the scalded milk gradually, stirring constantly. Cook over hot water for 20 minutes. Mix together the other ingredients, and add to the cornmeal mixture. Turn into a buttered 1½-quart baking dish and set in a pan of hot water. Bake at 350° for 1 hour. Yield: 6 servings.

Charlotte Russe

4   envelopes unflavored gelatin
7   cups milk, divided
8   egg yolks
1   cup sugar
1   tablespoon vanilla extract
8   egg whites, beaten very stiff
8   tablespoons sugar
1   cup thick cream
6   teaspoons sugar

Dissolve the gelatin in 1 cup of milk. Make a custard, using egg yolks, remaining 6 cups of milk, sugar, and vanilla. Add gelatin to the custard and remove from heat when custard just comes to a boil. (It will curdle if allowed to boil.)

Let cool, then place in refrigerator until it begins to congeal. Beat egg whites until very stiff, and add 8 tablespoons sugar. Beat until sugar is dissolved. Whip cream and add 6 teaspoons sugar. Remove mixture from refrigerator, and stir or beat until no lumps are left. Fold in egg whites, then cream mixture. Return to refrigerator for several hours. Yield: 8 to 10 servings.

Fresh Peach Crumble

½   cup all-purpose flour
¾   cup nonfat dry milk solids
3   tablespoons sugar
¼   teaspoon ground nutmeg
¼   teaspoon salt
1   teaspoon ground cinnamon
⅓   cup butter or margarine
3   cups sliced fresh peaches

Mix flour, nonfat dry milk solids, sugar, nutmeg, salt, and cinnamon. Cut butter or margarine in with pastry blender or two knifes until mixture is crumbly. Arrange fresh peach slices in shallow, well greased baking dish. Sprinkle with flour mixture. Bake covered at 350° about 25 minutes, or until peaches are tender. Remove cover, and bake for 10 minutes longer, or until crumbs are brown. Yield: 4 servings.

Virginia Fried Apples

Cook bacon at moderate temperature until crisp. Drain, and keep hot. Leave about 4 tablespoons drippings in the skillet. Fill with sliced, unpeeled apples and brown lightly. Sprinkle with sugar (½ cup per quart), cover, and cook slowly until tender. Remove cover and let apples brown and to cook off excess juice. Serve on a hot platter with bacon.

Molasses-Pecan Pie

3 eggs, beaten
¾ cup unsulphured molasses
¾ cup light corn syrup
2 tablespoons margarine or
   butter, melted
⅛ teaspoon salt
1 teaspoon vanilla extract
1 tablespoon all-purpose flour
1 cup pecans
1 unbaked 8-inch pie shell

Combine first six ingredients. Make a
paste of small amount of mixture and
flour; stir into remaining mixture. Add
pecans. Turn into unbaked shell. Bake
at 325° for 1 hour, or until firm. Yield:
1 (8-inch) pie.

Blackberry or Dewberry Cobbler

1 unbaked 10-inch double crust
4 to 6 cups very ripe blackberries
   or dewberries
1 cup sugar
¼ cup water
2 tablespoons all-purpose flour
¼ cup sugar
3 tablespoons butter

Make pastry; roll half very thin and use
it to line a 2-inch-deep baking pan. Roll
other half thin and cut into 2-inch
strips. Bake half the strips in a preheated
375° oven until lightly browned.

Put berries, 1 cup sugar, and water into
a saucepan. Cook until berries are soft.
Mix flour and ¼ cup sugar and add to
berries. Cook, stirring constantly until
mixture has thickened slightly. Spoon
berries into pastry-lined pan with cooked
pastry strips stirred throughout filling.
Dot with butter. Cover with remainder
of pastry strips (uncooked). Bake at
425° until pastry is brown. Yield:
1 (10-inch) pie.

Coconut Pie

½ cup sugar
⅓ cup all-purpose flour
3 egg yolks
2 cups milk, divided
¾ cup coconut
1 baked 9-inch pie shell
¼ teaspoon cream of tartar
3 egg whites
6 tablespoons sugar

Combine ½ cup sugar and flour in top
of double boiler. Beat egg yolks in
small bowl and add ¼ cup of milk.
Heat remaining 1¾ cups milk and add
to sugar and flour mixture; cook in top
of double boiler, stirring until it
thickens. Slowly add eggs and milk to
mixture, stirring constantly. Cook until it
thickens, stirring constantly. Add coconut and pour into a pie shell. Make
meringue by beating egg whites and
cream of tartar until stiff; add sugar
gradually and continue beating until it
holds a peak. Spread on pie and bake at
400° until brown. Yield: 1 (9-inch) pie.

Lemon Meringue Pie

1 cup sugar
⅓ cup cornstarch
1½ cups hot water
3 slightly beaten egg yolks
3 tablespoons butter
4 tablespoons freshly squeezed
   lemon juice
1⅓ tablespoons grated lemon rind
1 baked 9-inch pastry shell
   Meringue

Mix sugar and cornstarch thoroughly.
Gradually stir in hot water. Cook over
moderate heat, stirring constantly until
mixture boils. Boil for 1 minute or until
mixture thickens. Slowly stir half the
hot mixture into slightly beaten egg
yolks and then beat into hot mixture
in saucepan. Boil for 1 minute longer,

stirring constantly. Remove from heat and continue stirring until smooth. Blend in butter, lemon juice, and lemon rind. Return mixture to heat for 1 or 2 minutes, stirring constantly, until firm. Pour into baked pie shell and cover with Meringue.

Meringue

  3 egg whites
¼ teaspoon cream of tartar
  6 tablespoons sugar

Beat egg whites with cream of tartar until frothy. Gradually beat in sugar. Continue beating until stiff and glossy. Pile meringue onto pie filling. Seal to edge of crust to prevent shrinking. Bake at 400° until brown. Yield: 1 (9-inch) pie.

Buttermilk Pie

  3 eggs
  1 cup sugar
  2 tablespoons all-purpose flour
½ cup melted butter or margarine
  1 cup buttermilk
  1 teaspoon vanilla or lemon extract
  1 unbaked 9-inch pie shell

Beat eggs slightly and add sugar and flour. Then add melted butter or margarine and mix well. Add buttermilk and flavoring and pour into unbaked pie shell. Bake at 325° until custard is set. Yield: 1 (9-inch) pie.

Lemon Chess Pie

  2 cups sugar
½ cup butter or margarine
  5 eggs
  1 cup milk
  1 tablespoon all-purpose flour
  1 tablespoon cornmeal
¼ cup freshly squeezed lemon juice
    Grated rind of 3 large lemons
  1 unbaked 9-inch pie shell

Cream sugar and butter or margarine; add eggs and milk, beat well. Then add flour, cornmeal, lemon juice, and grated lemon rind. Pour mixture in the pan, baking at 350° until done. Yield: 1 (9-inch) pie.

Favorite Pecan Pie

  3 eggs
  1 cup white sugar
  1 cup dark corn syrup
  1 cup whole pecans
⅛ teaspoon salt
  1 teaspoon vanilla extract
  1 unbaked 9-inch pie shell
    Whipped cream (optional)

Beat eggs, sugar, and corn syrup together. Add pecans, salt, and vanilla. Pour into unbaked pie shell. Bake at 425° for 10 minutes, then reduce heat to 350° and complete baking in 25 to 30 minutes. Brush melted butter or margarine over pecans while the pie is hot. Serve pie slightly warm or cold, with or without whipped cream. Yield: 1 (9-inch) pie.

Sweet Potato Pie

  2 eggs
  1 cup sugar
  1 teaspoon salt
⅛ teaspoon ground nutmeg
  1 teaspoon ground cinnamon
  1 cup milk
  2 tablespoons butter or margarine
1½ cups cooked mashed sweet potatoes
  1 unbaked 8-inch pie shell

Beat the eggs slightly; add sugar, salt, spices, and milk. Add butter or margarine to mashed sweet potatoes and blend with milk and egg mixture. Pour into unbaked pie shell and bake at 450° for 10 minutes. Reduce heat to 350° and bake for 30 to 40 minutes or until filling is firm. Yield: 1 (8-inch) pie.

Never-Fail Pastry

    3 cups all-purpose flour
       Pinch salt
    1 cup vegetable shortening
    ½ cup cold water

Put flour and salt into large bowl. Cut in ½ cup shortening with two knives until mixture resembles cornmeal. Cut in the remaining shortening until the particles are about the size of navy beans. Sprinkle the water a little at a time over the surface. Blend by tossing with a fork until mixture leaves sides of bowl and forms a ball. Avoid stirring. Wrap in waxed paper and chill for about 30 minutes before rolling. Yield: 3 (8- or 9-inch) single crusts.

Deep-Fried Apple Pies

    3 cups sliced, peeled tart apples
    ½ cup water
    1 teaspoon freshly squeezed lemon juice
    ¼ cup sugar
    ½ teaspoon ground cinnamon
    ⅛ teaspoon ground nutmeg
       Pastry for double crust
       Vegetable shortening or cooking oil for deep frying
       Butter or margarine
       Powdered sugar

Put apples into a saucepan; add water and lemon juice. Cover tightly and cook over low heat for 15 minutes, or until tender. Remove apples and drain. Blend in sugar, cinnamon, and nutmeg.

Shape pastry into two balls. Using one ball at a time, flatten on a lightly floured surface and roll out ⅛ inch thick. Cut out rounds, using a 3½-inch cutter. Heat shortening or oil to 375°.

Place 2 tablespoons apple mixture on each pastry round; dot with butter or margarine. Moisten half of the edge of each round with water. Fold the other half of round over filling. Press edges together with a fork to seal tightly.

Lower pies into hot shortening or oil. Deep-fry for about 3 minutes or until golden brown. Turn pies as they rise to surface and several times during cooking. Do not pierce.

Remove pies from shortening and drain over frying pan for a few seconds before removing onto absorbent paper. Sprinkle with powdered sugar; serve warm. Yield: 15 fried pies.

Sweet Potato Crust

    1 cup sifted all-purpose flour
    1 teaspoon baking powder
    ½ teaspoon salt
    1 cup mashed cooked sweet potatoes
    ⅓ cup melted butter
    1 egg, well beaten

Sift flour, measure, add baking powder and salt, and sift again. Work in mashed sweet potatoes, melted butter, and egg. Roll ¼ inch thick and use as cover for chicken or meat deep dish pie. Yield: pastry for 1 (9-inch) crust.

Old World Apple Pie

    2 cups finely chopped tart apples
    ¾ cup sugar
    2 tablespoons all-purpose flour
    ⅓ teaspoon salt
    1 egg, beaten
    ½ teaspoon vanilla extract
    1 cup commercial sour cream
    1 unbaked 9-inch pie shell

Peel and chop apples and set aside. Combine sugar, flour and salt; add egg, vanilla, and sour cream. Beat until smooth. Add apples, mix well, and pour into pastry-lined piepan. Bake at 375° for 15 minutes; reduce heat to 325° and bake 30 minutes longer. Remove from oven and sprinkle with Topping.

Topping

⅓ cup all-purpose flour
¼ cup butter
⅓ cup brown sugar

Combine ingredients and blend well. Sprinkle over baked pie. Return pie to oven and bake at 325° for 20 minutes or until topping is brown. Yield: 1 (9-inch) pie.

Almond Pastry

1½ cups all-purpose flour
¼ cup ground almonds
¼ cup sugar
¼ teaspoon salt
½ cup shortening
1 egg, beaten
Cold water

Mix the first four ingredients and cut in the shortening. Add beaten egg and enough cold water to make a stiff dough. Chill thoroughly and line a 9-inch pieplate. Yield: pastry for 1 (9-inch) crust.

Blackberry Pie

2½ cups canned blackberries, drained
1 cup blackberry juice
3 tablespoons tapioca
Sugar to sweeten
Pastry for 9-inch pie

Combine drained blackberries, juice, tapioca, and sugar. Let stand for 15 minutes, or while pastry is being made. Line pan with pastry; add blackberries and cover with strips of pastry. Bake until pastry is browned. Yield: 1 (9-inch) pie.

Peach Cobbler

3½ cups cooked sliced peaches
½ cup sugar
1½ tablespoons cornstarch
½ teaspoon salt
1 tablespoon butter or margarine
¼ teaspoon almond extract
Pastry for single crust

Drain syrup from peaches, and place peaches in a 9-inch pieplate or 1-quart baking dish. Measure 1 cup of the syrup and heat. Blend sugar, cornstarch, and salt; stir into hot syrup. Cook and stir until mixture boils. Stir in butter or margarine and almond extract. Pour over peaches. Roll pastry thin and cut in ½-inch strips. Arrange lattice fashion over top of baking dish. Bake at 400° for about 35 minutes, or until pastry is well browned. Serve warm. Yield: 1 (9-inch) pie.

Raisin Pie

2½ cups seedless raisins
1½ cups water
¾ cup white corn syrup
2 tablespoons all-purpose flour
2 tablespoons sugar
Juice and grated rind of 1 lemon
½ cup chopped nuts
1 unbaked 9-inch double crust

Combine raisins and water and boil for about 10 minutes. Combine white corn syrup, flour, sugar, lemon rind, and juice. Add to raisins, stir well, and let cook for 2 to 3 minutes. Add chopped nuts and let cool.

Pour cooled filling into unbaked pie shell. Cover with lattice strips of pastry, if desired. Bake at 400° for 10 minutes, reduce heat to 350° and bake for 20 to 30 minutes longer. Yield: 1 (9-inch) pie.

Jellymaking Hints

When making jelly, it is better to prepare small amounts at one cooking. Do not double recipe.

The biggest problem when making jelly without added pectin is to know when the jelly is done.

A jelly thermometer is the most accurate way of testing jelly. To do this, test your thermometer in boiling water to see what temperature is recorded. Jelly should be cooked to 8° above the boiling point of water (220°). For an accurate thermometer reading, have the thermometer in a vertical position and read it at eye level. Bulb of the thermometer should be completely covered with the jelly mixture after it comes to a full rolling boil.

The spoon or sheet test may also be used, although it is not as accurate as the thermometer test. Dip a cold metal spoon in the boiling jelly mixture. Then raise it at least a foot above the kettle, out of the steam, and turn the spoon so the syrup runs off the side. If the syrup forms two drops that flow together and fall off the spoon as one sheet, the jelly should be done.

Fresh Strawberry Jelly

2½ quarts fresh strawberries
  1 (2½-ounce) package powdered pectin
¼ teaspoon salt
  5 cups sugar

Crush strawberries; put through a jelly bag and squeeze out juice. There should be 3½ cups of juice. If there is a shortage of juice, add a little water to the pulp, and squeeze out again. Mix pectin with the juice and bring to a rapid boil. Add salt and sugar and boil hard for 1 minute, stirring constantly. Remove from heat. Skim off foam. Pour at once into hot, sterilized jars, leaving ½ inch space at top of each. Seal immediately.

Berry Jelly

4 cups berry juice
3 cups sugar

Carefully wash and drain berries. Select half of the berries that are just red and the other half fully ripe. Place in large kettle and crush. Bring to a boil and boil slowly for 5 to 15 minutes, stirring occasionally. Let stand for 10 minutes. Drain. Measure juice into a large kettle and place on heat. Bring juice to a boil and add sugar. Stir only until sugar is dissolved. Cook very rapidly until jelly stage is reached. Strain through a layer of damp cheesecloth and pour immediately into hot, sterilized jelly glasses or jars to ¼ inch of the top. Seal jars immediately. Cover jelly glasses with a thin cloth and allow to remain covered overnight. Then remove cloth and cover jelly with melted paraffin; seal; and store in a cool, dry place.

Citrus Marmalade

  Peel of ½ grapefruit
  Peel of 1 orange
  Peel of 1 lemon
4 cups cold water
2 cups boiling water
3 cups sugar
1 cup grapefruit juice
1¾ cups orange juice
⅓ cup freshly squeezed lemon juice

Wash the fruit and extract juice. Remove membrane from inside the peel. Cut peel into very thin strips. Add cold water to the peel and simmer slowly in a covered pan until tender, for about 30 minutes. Drain off and discard the liquid; add boiling water to the peel. Add the sugar and boil rapidly to 220°, about 20 minutes. Add the fruit juices and cook again to the same temperature, about 25 minutes, stirring frequently.

Remove from heat; skim and stir alternately for 5 minutes. Ladle marmalade into hot, sterilized jars and seal at once.

Pear Mincemeat

    4 quarts ground pears
    2 (1-pound) boxes seedless raisins
    4 pounds sugar
    2 lemons
 1½ teaspoons salt
    3 teaspoons ground cinnamon
    1 teaspoon ground allspice
    1 teaspoon ground cloves

Mix all ingredients. Cook in large kettle until tender. Pour into hot, sterilized jars and seal.

Watermelon Rind Preserves

    1 pound watermelon cubes
    8 cups water
    2 tablespoons household lime
    2 cups sugar
    4 cups water
 ½ lemon, sliced

Select melons that have thick rind. Trim off the outer green skin and the pink flesh, and use only the greenish-white parts of the rind. Cut the rind into ½- or 1-inch cubes, and weigh. Then soak the cubes for 3½ hours in lime water (2 quarts water and 2 tablespoons lime from hardware store). Next, drain and place the cubes in clear water for 1 hour. Again, drain off the water and boil for 1½ hours after fresh water has been added, then drain again. Make a syrup of 2 cups sugar and 1 quart water. Add rind and boil for 1 hour. As the syrup thickens, add ½ lemon, thinly sliced,

for each pound of fruit. When the syrup begins to thicken and when the melon is clear, the preserves are ready for the jars. Pack the preserves into hot, sterilized jars, add enough syrup to cover, and seal.

Pickled Okra

    Garlic (1 clove for each jar)
    Hot peppers (1 for each jar)
    Okra
    Dill seed (1 teaspoon for each jar)
    1 *quart white vinegar*
    1 *cup water*
 ½ *cup salt*

Place the garlic and hot pepper in the bottom of hot, sterilized pint jars. Pack firmly with clean, young okra pods from which only part of the stem has been removed. Stem end must be open. Add dill seed.

After packing jars, bring vinegar, water, and salt to a boil. Simmer for about 5 minutes and pour, while boiling hot, over the okra. Seal the jars immediately. This amount of pickling solution will fill from 5 to 7 pint jars.

Old-Fashioned Peach Preserves

Wash, scald, pit, peel, and cut firm, ripe peaches. Weigh. Mix equal amounts of sugar with prepared fruit; let stand overnight in a cool place and then cook (without adding water) until the fruit is tender and syrup is thick. Pour into hot, sterilized jars and seal.

Variations

Add 2 cracked peach seed, or 2 drops almond extract, or ¼ teaspoon vanilla extract for variety.